SHRUBS

For Everyone

PETER SEABROOK

floraprint

First published 1997 by
Burall Floraprint Limited, Wisbech, UK

Copyright © Peter Seabrook and Burall Floraprint Limited, 1997

A CIP catalogue record for this book is available from the British Library

ISBN 0 903001 71 3

Floraprint books are published by Burall Floraprint Limited, Wisbech, UK

Picture Credits
All photographs by the author or from the Floraprint collection with the following exceptions:
Harry Smith Collection, page 27
Photos Great Britain, cover inset, pages 3, 13
Photos Horticultural, pages 16, 24, 25, 26, 66

Cover photograph: *Pyracantha Orange Glow* and *Parthenoscissus Veitchii*
Back photographs, top: *Hydrangea petiolaris*; bottom: *Lonicera tellmanniana*
Page 1 and chapter pages: *Paeonia suffruticosa*

Edited, indexed and typeset by Jane Robinson

Printed in Singapore

Foreword

Peter Seabrook, the horticulturist who is known to millions of television viewers and readers of his national newspaper, magazine columns and books started to grow plants as a school boy for the sheer joy of it and has continued to do so ever since.

His first job as a nursery hand started well before leaving school after which he trained at Writtle College to gain the College Diploma and the Royal Horticultural Society National Diploma in Horticulture. After more than twenty years working full-time in the nursery and garden centre industries he has since shared his time between busy commercial interests as director and advisor to various leading nursery, garden centre and horticultural retail chains and horticultural journalism.

Most people will however know Peter Seabrook publicly from his British television broadcasts on BBC1 and BBC2 over the past twenty five years in such programmes as Gardeners' World, the Chelsea Flower Show, Pebble-Mill-At-One, The Really Useful Show, Gardeners' Direct Line and Peter Seabrook's Gardening Week. In the United States of America and Canada he is well-known for his regular appearances over the the past twenty years on the Victory Garden programme produced by WGBH-TV, Boston.

Each year he travels many thousands of miles round the world and meets thousands of gardeners when undertaking speaking engagements, visiting gardens and nurseries. This provides a clear insight into the needs of the home gardener. Whatever spare time he has, Peter continues to cultivate his own small suburban garden. This free-time gardening is a constant reminder of the wishes and desires of the ordinary home owner and helps to keep his feet firmly on the ground.

He hopes the very real pleasure to be gained from gardening and cultivating ornamental plants will be realised by more people as a result of the advice in this book – some of which has been set to music by Anthony Bremner in a cantata called 'In The Shrubbery'. It is available in a track on 'The Green CD' (Tall Poppies TP064) performed by The Song Company and Friends.

Acknowledgements

The author expresses his thanks to all those in the nursery and garden centre trade who have been so hlepful over the years spent gathering material for this book. He is also indebted to photographers Ed Gabriel and Michael Warren; to Tony Bremner whose cantata 'In the shrubbery' sets some of this book to music; to Margaret his wife without whose patience and hard work this and previous books would never have seen the light of day and to his editor Jane Robinson who did such a good job against very tight production schedules.

Solanum jasminoides

Clematis 'Jackmanii'

Cornus florida 'Cherokee Chief'

Contents

Introduction

Easily grown woody perennial plants, ranging from 20cm low shrubs to small trees are available in a tremendous range of form, colour and fragrance. There are types to suit every situation, both formal garden layouts and natural settings. No patch of soil is either too large or too small to accommodate examples of these popular plants. Indeed even the smallest patio or yard can be improved by using shrubs in containers such as tubs and troughs.

Suitable varieties can be found for every site and soil type.

For many people shrubbery conjures up dense woody growth 2–3m high, overcrowded, dark and far from attractive. It is not until we stop to think about the value of shrubs in gardens that their adaptable nature and useful role is fully appreciated.

Dowdy and dusty old shrubberies are too common because planting has been done carelessly, without the all important time spent on planning –

that is choosing the right kinds for the right place and space. These errors at the outset are made worse by neglecting even the small amount of attention that shrubs required.

For a mixed shrub border your selection could include all the qualities that shrubs possess. Low growing and ground covering plants would be used at the front of the border, taller shrubs at the back. Evergreens and attractive bark furnish the garden in winter. Your choice could include a succession of flowers throughout the year or selections to give attractive features in spring or autumn.

Quite apart from the accepted role in borders, as an attractive feature in their own right, and in beds to provide protection, privacy and a pleasant vista, shrubs are adaptable to many garden uses. We have the many climbing and clinging plants that are excellent on fences and for screening, the varieties which tolerate clipping to form hedges and informal barriers, shrubs suited to restricted root growth for troughs and tubs, as well as wall plants and ground cover subjects.

Carefully planted, a number of shrubs quickly spread over the ground and smother out weeds to provide easy gardening with very little annual maintenance. They are especially useful in this form to furnish banks where they help to hold the soil in place as well as providing complete ground cover. Choose the dwarf lavenders for sunny banks and light soil to provide flowers and fragrance as well as the silver-grey foliage. The long-flowering potentillas also do well

Spiraea vanhouttei has cascading branches full of flower

Introduction

Mixed shrub border – cytisus and spiraea

in such places. Where the soil is heavier and the site less sunny the evergreen Cotoneasters are excellent ground cover plants.

A lot of different shrubs can be used to provide hedges and screens, from the lowest evergreen *Euonymus* and Buxus to the 6m and taller laurel (*Prunus laurocerasus*) and *Cotoneaster lacteus*. A number of the popular flowering shrubs such as the flowering currant (*Ribes*) and *Forsythia* also form good hedges.

Walls and fences have become a dominant feature of our modern small gardens and once again shrubs in free-standing, climbing and clinging forms are perfect plants to clad and soften them. Even where there is no soil most shrubs can be grown in tubs and containers, at least for a few years. Plants as varied as Japanese maples, *Hydrangea*, *Camellia* and *Wisteria* respond well to pot culture.

It will be seen from this short introduction that shrubs have many uses and no garden or patio should be

without them to provide attractive foliage, pretty flowers, fragrance, stems to cut and berries for decoration and to feed birds. There are countless

different kinds to choose from and, as can be seen from the illustrations in this book, many of them are of outstanding beauty.

Lonicera x tellmanniana bringing colour to bare, wooden rails

Putting Shrubs To Use

Many plants are bought on impulse because they look nice at the time and then are used as random fillers for gaps in borders. You will get much more from your plantings if a little thought is given to how any purchase, or plant you have raised, can best be used.

IN GARDEN DESIGN

While the selection of shrubs will vary widely with personal likes and dislikes, most planting will contain both deciduous and evergreen subjects. The evergreens, by holding their foliage all the year round, have obvious advantages for screening, furnishing the garden in winter, deflecting noise and filtering wind to provide shelter.

Deciduous plants, in contrast, have bare branches throughout the dormant season but more than compensate for this with their fresh new growth in spring followed by the verdant canopy in summer and the kaleidoscope of autumn colour before leaf fall.

Foliage is but one of the decorative tools, equally important are the beauty and interest of bark and twigs and the colour and fragrance of flowers and fruits. All the qualities of each shrub need consideration when forming a collection or planning a planting scheme.

Coloured barks and unusual forms adopted by the branches of some shrubs are worthy of greater attention, especially to add interest to the garden in winter. The bright red and yellow bark of "Dogwood" and willow and the twisted stems of hazel are good examples.

Thought should be given to the background for such plants: dark evergreens contrast with the bright barks; silver or golden evergreens provide the means of highlighting corkscrewed and twisted branches.

Fragrance is considered in two forms, the heady air-filling perfume of the more strongly scented, like *Philadelphus*, lilac, honeysuckle and deciduous azaleas and the more subtle scents requiring knowledge and close attention to savour and appreciate. For example the need to crush rosemary and chequerberry leaves between the fingers, to bruise sage and the flowers of some lavender cultivars and to visit some sweetbriar roses after rain.

Shrubs are marvellous providers of flowers, foliage and fruits for indoor decoration. Remember this when you have difficulty accommodating fully grown shrubs in any one position. The chances are with such plants as *camellia*, holly, *mahonia*, *senecio* and *pittosporum* for example, regular gathering for flower arrangement will restrict their size.

The autumn glory of Parthenocissus creates a living wall out of this lifeless framework

Pyracantha 'Orange Glow' completely disguises this functional garage

Use slow-growing trailing plants such as this Cotoneaster microphyllus to provide added interest to low garden walls

Fragrance from Philadelphus, above, or from honeysuckle and lilac brings an added dimension to garden design.

IN CONTAINERS

Paved areas and small patio gardens are filled with summer colour and then all too often ignored from October to March. Where a framework of shrubs, including a good proportion of evergreens, is grown in pots such areas can be made very attractive the year round. Indeed the shrub collection will also save money in reducing the number of summer annuals which need to be either bought or raised each spring.

Good choices include *camellia, fatsia, osmanthus* and *skimmia*. These all grow well in pots and tubs, are evergreen, flower in the October to March period and all but the *fatsia* and some camellias have fragrant flowers. *Fatsia* and *skimmia* are especially suited to partially-shaded

Rhododendrons make a showy display in this wooden barrel

Contrasting foliage provided by container grown plants bring this private corner to life

summer and then rich autumn leaf colours, plus edible fruits, deciduous azaleas, all the dwarf *Euonymus*, red-leaved and berried *Berberis thunbergia* 'Helmond Pillar', bamboos and of course hydrangeas, wisterias, all the Japanese Acers and *Acer negundo* 'Variegatum'.

Where you have some space out of sight, grow a few shrubs in containers for their showy flowers, even if their attractive season is relatively short. Then when they are leafless and unattractive a swap can be made with evergreens from the standing out area. Given this luxury of space the large flowered tree paeonies and mop head hydrangeas are very colourful in May and July/August respectively.

I would particularly recommend container shrub gardening to those home owners with a small paved yard. Grow one small tree or tall shrub, such as *wisteria*, up on a trunk to give height and then group the rest around and beneath it.

Choose the largest containers you can handle and accommodate, putting the largest on a small wheeled plinth makes moving them to allow sweeping up leaves so much easier. Use a mixture of half and half John Innes Potting Compost No 3 and all-peat potting compost. In very exposed positions, where wind will blow taller plants over, choose wide-based containers and all John Innes No 3 for added weight.

All containers must have holes in the base for free drainage, this is very important in winter with shrubs such as Japanese Acers killed by waterlogging rather than cold. All will need regular watering and feeding and automatic trickle irrigation lines cannot be recommended enough for spring to autumn use. Where such systems are introduced the quality of growth is always so much better and they are essential if the home owner is away for some days in summer.

Life expectancy can be considerably extended by careful root pruning in the

places and all these evergreens will take some shade.

Walking through garden centre container plant areas and seeing the enormous range of shrubs grown these days in pots, there is obviously no shortage of choice. Over recent years I have been surprised how many of them grow and perform well in large pots. A collection of half a dozen or so can be repeatedly rearranged with the changing seasons to bring each one to the fore in its best season.

Among popular kinds which have served me well are: *magnolia*, both M. *stellata* and M. x *soulangeana* (grown in tubs for a few years, these develop into free-flowering specimens for subsequent garden planting), *Cotoneaster sternianus*, which has a very elegant habit, really sharp leaf outline and free-berrying habit, *Prunus triloba* with lovely fresh green leaves in late spring, blueberries for their jade-green flowers, good green

Grouping containers together looks more attractive than single pots standing at random

Callistemon citrinus needs tender loving care which can easily be provided if grown in a container and moved under glass in winter

This well established planting of ivy and box provides a half-way step between garden and house

dormant season and replacing some of the old compost with new: a scaled-up bonsai treatment.

Feeding is most easily done by applying slow release fertiliser granules once or twice a year in spring and summer. Where growth is not as fast as required and the leaf size is small, diluted liquid feeding will rapidly improve things.

AS HEDGES

They might need once- or twice-yearly trimming but once established, hedges and living screens are as much a part of a good garden as lawns and flower beds. An evergreen laurel hedge is a shining embellishment to any garden year-round. The changing leaf colour of beech, from new spring growth to old leaf colour when they fall twelve months later, is a joy to behold.

We can hardly berate farmers for pulling out hedges and then leave our plots denuded of them. They provide marvellous cover – and food in the case of berried plants – for birds and wildlife. Get a good hedge established and unlike wooden fences there will be no fear of it blowing down in gales.

Don't be afraid of trying shrubs not usually thought of as hedging material, especially for less formal use. *Aucuba*, *garrya*, *hibiscus*, dwarf lilac, *senecio*, *Viburnum tinus* are some likely kinds which immediately come to mind. I saw a magnificent two metre high hedge of camellias in New Zealand.

Patience is the key to success, especially in the first year or two. Good soil preparation and careful planting is needed to get the main branch framework established. The planting sequence for a long row is to take soil from the first hole right down the line to the last site. Soil from the second hole can then be used to plant the first hedge plant, soil from the third to the second planting, and so on, right down the row.

Where balled specimens of such

When pruned, Prunus laurocerasus makes a strong, evergreen hedge.

good evergreens as *Berberis* x *stenophylla*, yew, holly and box are used, transplanting is best done in September/October and March/April. All bare root deciduous plants will need to be planted during the dormant season, from October to February, but when the soil is unfrozen. Container plants can of course be set out at any time the soil is neither frozen nor waterlogged.

Be sure to keep them all well watered during dry weather in their early years, especially strong-growing subjects such as flowering currant, *forsythia*, *escallonia* and *laurel*.

Berberis thunbergia 'Atropurpurea Nana' makes a neat and colourful low growing hedge

Putting shrubs to use

Hedging Tip

Plant strong-growing plants such as beech and quickthorn at a 45° angle. The shoots then grow along the stem rather than from the tip and this increases the number of basal branches. A double row forms a more dense and impenetrable hedge.

IN THE HOME

Several hardy evergreen shrubs make useful houseplants, particularly for places which are cool and rather dark in winter. The obvious example is small leaved ivy (*hedera*) either used as a trailing plant or trained over some form of support.

The all-green leaved cultivars will put up with the least amount of light and even the variegated kinds, which grow very little in low winter temperatures, will do a good decorating job for several months. Small leaved ivies grafted onto stems of *fatshedera* to form weeping standards provide something a little different in form.

Other shrub contenders for houseplant and cool conservatory use include: *aucuba*, bay, *camellia*, *fatsia* and *pernettya*. The *fatsia*, (false castor oil plant) is especially adaptable and succeeds in a wide range of temperatures. Where they go above 50°f (10°c) the leaves grow rather soft and will need slow aclimatisation if they are to be moved outside for the summer.

Pernettya and some skimmias have been grown commercially for indoor use rather like the better known Winter Cherry (*Solanum capsicastrum*). Large batches of young female plants are grown with a few specimen males to provide pollination outside all summer. When well berried they are brought indoors and used in window boxes for winter decoartion. These shrubs unlike the *solanum* are unlikely to drop their colourful fruits.

Flower-filled stems of Chaenomeles make good, long lasting cut flowers

An informal arrangement, here using lilac, brings the freshness of outdoors into the living room

PLANNING A BORDER

While our artist has taken full artistic licence here, presenting for example *choisya* and *buddleia* in full flower at the same time, the illustration does show how different shrub shapes can be used to their best effect. Contrasting the spiralling shoots of variegated *berberis* (middle left side) with the bold leaves and heavy heads of *hydrangea* is the kind of placement to be recommended.

Gardeners are well advised to draw up imaginary borders for their own plants before setting out to make purchases. Arrangements of the type drawn here could either be duplicated to form a circular bed with the taller *hibiscus* and *buddleia* to the centre or sited against a wall or fence with taller plants at the back.

It will often be necessary to have a group of several of each of the smaller-growing kinds in the foreground. Planted as singles, they get dwarfed and lost against the more vigorous and taller-growing kinds. A bold skirt of *lavender*, for example, not only provides colourful and fragrant flowers in summer but bright silver-grey foliage the year round. One could argue that all the taller plants here are deciduous and would therefore look empty and sparse for the winter. Swapping the tallest *hibiscus* with *Viburnum tinus* would correct this and increase the flower bud colour in winter.

Additional flower colour could be added to the taller shrubs by under-planting with *clematis* and a similar arrangement made with *Clematis macropetala* scrambling through the

lower-growing shrubs to the front of your border.

Our deliberate mistake could be the *pieris* (centre right), not just because the new red shoots come mainly in spring but more for its soil requirements. Most of the remaining shrubs chosen here grow in neutral to slightly alkaline soil, whereas the *pieris* needs acid conditions.

Rather like making up a jigsaw, each shrub is one piece to be fitted carefully to form the whole picture. Height, spread, flowering time and colour, leaf type and soil requirements all have to be considered. Don't expect absolute perfection, choose the shrubs you like and then carefully adjust, pruning to restrain size and varying the soil somewhat – digging in peat, for example, to make it more acid – to achieve your objective.

We read often enough recommendations and schemes for summer bedding and herbaceous borders and there is no reason why you should not do exactly the same for shrubs. It just takes fewer plants and you are planting on a grander scale, with the planting likely to remain in place for many years. Most of us make mistakes, there's no harm in digging them out and replacing with something more suitable.

Taking one shrub out can leave something of a hole but you will be amazed how quickly the replacement fills in and surrounding shrubs fill out. Don't be afraid if your plants on paper come to look very sparse when planted, just take a photograph after planting and at yearly intervals for two or three years – you'll find the changes from year to year unbelievable.

Making Your Choice

Selecting the kind of shrub you would like to grow is only part of the path to success. Consideration should also be given to the physical qualities of each one when bought and the site preparation needed to get it to grow well.

BUYING YOUR PLANT

The introduction of widescale "container growing" of woody perennials in the early 1960s revolutionised shrub gardening and made it much easier to get and establish a very wide range of different kinds. Given a good supply of pot-grown plants, transplanting can be undertaken at any time of the year as long as the soil is neither waterlogged nor frozen.

We now have four main options open to us when it comes to obtaining plants:

1. Bare root deciduous shrubs; lifted from the field and moved from the place where they were propagated and grown with the roots free of soil. Field growing and moving without soil costs less but the inevitable damage to roots when lifting increases the transplanting check. Where the bare roots are kept moist by surrounding them with damp moss, peat or straw and the plants are quickly replanted – ideally between October and December and certainly before bud burst in spring – re-establishment is good for most plants. A few, such as brooms (*Cytisus*) and fire–thorn (*Pyracantha*) do not withstand root damage and need to be pot grown.

2. Balled evergreen and deciduous shrubs, lifted from the field again but here with most of the soil retained on and around the main root framework and held firmly in place. Burlap or hessian (open-weave material such as sacking) is used to hold the soil in place and allows transplanting with a minimum of root disturbance. Where the hessian is a natural material that rots in the soil, it can be left in place. More recently sheet plastic and non-rot man-made fabrics are also used to

hold the root ball together and these will need to be removed when planting.

3. Root wrapped – rootainered or containerised (as opposed to container grown) evergreen and deciduous shrubs – this being the compromise between 1 and 2 above. The shrubs are lifted with as much root as possible, the soil very gently removed and replaced by a peat-based planting compost. Polythene bag pots and sheet polythene are used to hold

A comparison of trees and shrubs, and bare-rooted, balled and root-wrapped specimens

SHRUBS

FOR FRAGRANCE
Azalea
Chimonanthes
Choisya ternata
Daphne mezereum
Elaeagnus x ebbingei
Hamamelis
Jasmine officinale
Lavandula
Lonicera
Magnolia
Mahonia 'Charity'
Philadelphus 'Virginal'
Rosa
Syringa vulgaris cultivars
Viburnum carlesii

FOR GROUND COVER
Cotoneaster, for example *dammeri*
Cytisus x kewensis
Euonymus radicans cultivars
Gaultheria procumbens
Hebe rakaiensis (syn. *subalpina*)
Hedera species
Hypericum calycinum
Prunus laurocerasus 'Otto Luyken'

FOR STEEP BANKS
Cotoneaster, e.g. 'Skogholm'
Cytisus praecox
Hedera colchica
Lavandula spica
Potentilla fruticosa
Spiraea x bumalda

the compost in place but also elastic netting surrounds them. The netting alone can be left in place because it allows roots to grow through but pots and the like must be removed when planting.

4. Container plants, here both evergreen and deciduous shrubs are grown in pots of various sizes and can be transplanted in all four seasons with virtually no root disturbance and no check to plant growth.

Lavandula spica 'Hidcote' providing low, scented ground cover

Spiraea japonica 'Little Princess'

GENERAL POINTS TO REMEMBER WHEN BUYING YOUR PLANTS

Container, balled and rootainer shrubs are heavy and as a result mail order carriage charges can be costly. For this reason it is usually cheaper to purchase from a local nursery or garden centre. The garden centre also allows for personal choice of well-shaped, vigorously growing specimens. Where less common plants are required it may be necessary to place orders with either the garden centre or reputable specialist mail order companies. Cheap offers and low-priced plants are all too often either inferior varieties, or diseased plants that are likely to prove to be a bad buy. The exception here is the very young plants (sometimes called "liners") and this may be the choice where the budget is small and the gardener is prepared to wait the extra years to see the shrub reach a decorative size. The fair price of really good plants is, however, an investment which will continue to grow in value.

WHAT ABOUT SIZE AND GROWTH?

Speed of growth and eventual height and spread will vary according to district, soil, situation and cultural care. The vital statistics listed in this book are the averages reached under normal garden condition. It should be remembered that plants growing in shade may be drawn up, that warm positions, high rainfall and rich soils will speed growth and can increase ultimate size. Equally, cold and dry positions and impoverished soil will restrict the size and speed of growth.

Bright sunlight, therefore south-facing slopes, will provide the brightest-coloured leaves of silver and golden variegated plants. Remember however some yellow- and cream-leaved shrubs can scorch in hot sunlight. Shady sites and rich soils,

This Cytisus kewensis grown on a stem could be used to provide height at the back of a border

Hydrangea petiolaris is suitably used climbing up, and trailing over this wall

FOR AUTUMN COLOUR

Acer palmatum
Amelanchier canadensis
Azalea luteum
Berberis
Euonymus europaeus
Leycesteria formosa
Rhus typhina
Ribes odoratum
Viburnum opulus

FOR WINTER FLOWERS

Camellia sasanqua
Chimonanthes praecox
Cornus mas
Erica carnea
Garrya elliptica
Hamamelis mollis
Jasminum nudiflorum
Viburnum farreri

FOR BERRIES AND FRUITS

Callicarpa bodinieri
Chaenomeles speciosa
Cotoneaster
Hippophae rhamnoides
Ilex
Pernettya
Pyracantha
Rosa moyesii
Skimmia japonica

FOR HOT DRY SITES

Berberis species
Caryopteris x clandonensis
Cytisus
Genista hispanica
Lavandula
Perovskia atriplicifolia
Santolina
Senecio greyi
Spartium junceum

FOR SHADE

Aucuba japonica
Euonymus radicans cultivars
Hydrangea petiolaris
Ilex species
Mahonia aquifolium
Rhododendron
Virburnum tinus

high in nitrogen, are likely to reduce the brightness of variegation and reduce the amount of flower. When the ultimate heights are known, mixed groups can be planted in such a way that they grow in balance one with another. Like an artist using colour, each selected plant is used to build up the complete but ever-changing picture.

This is the enthralling part of gardening: a continual challenge offering something of beauty and interest every day. If small plants are used at the outset, groups of each can be planted for quick effect and thinned as they increase in size and require more space.

Vigorous young plants will often establish themselves after transplanting more quickly than larger specimens that suffer a more severe check when moved. Furthermore, young plants retain the vigour of youth, often growing away fast enough to overtake larger plants of the same kind. This fact needs bearing in mind where a large area of new garden is to be planted and costs are a serious consideration. Younger, smaller plants will cost less than larger, older equivalents.

Groups of three, five and larger odd numbers are preferred, a single plant being left perhaps to remain as the final specimen when thinning has been completed. Compared with the cost of site preparation, building materials, wages, cultivation and planting the actual plants are a small part of the total price of making a garden.

The use of more, smaller plants will give a well-established look faster and quickly provide a mature appearance. Three plants, to be thinned down to one finally, may well cover the ground in a season and save two whole seasons of fortnightly hoeing for weed control where only one plant was used from the outset.

Trees on a clear stem give height to borders. Taller and upright-growing shrubs can similarly be used to the centre and back of any planting. Use weeping or trailing shrubs to flow over low walls and cover banks.

Ground-hugging prostrate plants can be used to cover the ground beneath larger specimens. A number of evergreen shrubs described in the following chapters can be used in this way. Many ground coverers are attractive in their own right but additionally make gardening easier by smothering weeds and ultimately require very little maintenance. One plant of *Cotoneaster dammeri*, for example, will give a metre or two of attractive year-round ground cover.

Try using four of these prostrate plants to form a skirt around a more upright-growing shrub. Evergreen cotoneasters beneath and around *Hibiscus* or *Euonymus radicans* cultivars around upright *Berberis*, or small-leaved ivy around *Hypericum* 'Hidcote' are good examples.

Bright sunlight provides the brightest coloured leaves of silver and golden variegated plants.

GETTING TO GRIPS WITH NAMES

The long Latin names of plants are a frightening obstacle to the gardening newcomer and too many of us create a complete and yet quite unnecessary mental block from the start. This is a great pity because these names are useful in breaking language barriers and in providing information about the plant once a few simple terms are understood.

From the tongue-twisting name *Acer palmatum* 'Dissectum Atropurpureum', one of the maples, we can decipher that the leaves are palm-shaped (palmatum), finely cut (Dissectum) and deep purple in colour. It is easy to get to know the terms and before long the meanings of words like *praecox* – early flowering – will be remembered. A catalogue of plant names provides a considerable amount of information about the plants. Leaf shape, size and colour, flower form and size of plants are but some of the qualities included in shrub names.

Common names in the native tongue, whilst instantly appealing, create confusion. In some cases one name is applied to two or more quite different plants by people in different localities. Additionally, newly introduced plants will have no common name. To avoid confusion all gardeners and nurserymen need to use the same name.

There is nothing more disheartening than to cultivate a desired plant only to find on flowering and fruiting that it is not what was wanted. Even worse is the purchase of two allegedly different plants to find that they differ only in name.

Shrubs are classified by botanists, in the same way as all other plants, according to flower type into large groups called families. The family name is not likely to be of any great importance to gardeners and is not included in the title by which we refer to each kind.

Genera. The plural of genus,

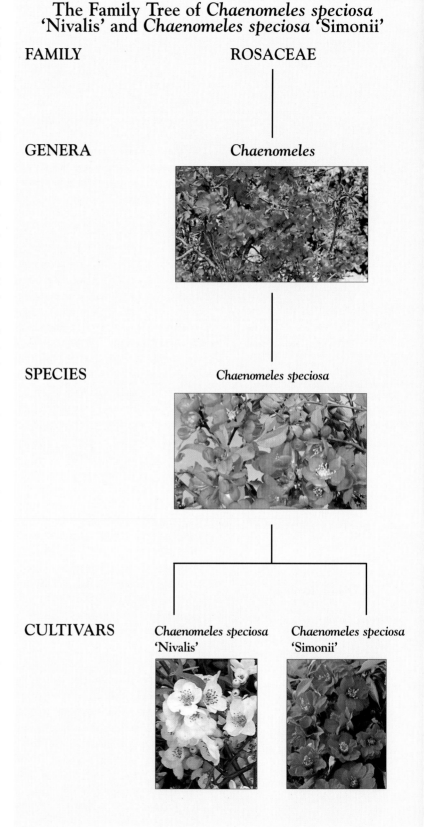

The Family Tree of *Chaenomeles speciosa* 'Nivalis' and *Chaenomeles speciosa* 'Simonii'

FAMILY   ROSACEAE

GENERA   *Chaenomeles*

SPECIES   *Chaenomeles speciosa*

CULTIVARS   *Chaenomeles speciosa* 'Nivalis'   *Chaenomeles speciosa* 'Simonii'

AWARD OF GARDEN MERIT

Where shrubs are of garden merit gardeners are helped in their assessment and choice of shrubs by The Royal Horticultural Society's Award of Garden Merit. Experienced members of the Society's committees continue to assess the full range of plants available to gardeners.

The plants are assessed at trials on the Society's gardens, at specialist collections throughout Britain and from the assessors' own collective experience.

The plants have to meet the following requirements before receiving the Award:

- *Excellent for ordinary garden use*
- *Good constitution*
- *Generally not susceptible to pests and diseases*
- *Do not require special conditions*
- *Distinct and stable forms*

The Award is often signified in catalogues and labels with this sign and on garden centres with a bed card.

It should be noted, however, that plants with good qualities and perhaps one minor weakness may be passed over, but remains well worth growing. For example, *Hedera helix* 'Goldheart' occasionally produces stems which revert to green and for this reason the AGM has been withdrawn from it. Where the gardener prunes out the reverted stems it remains one of our most decorative small-leaved dark green and yellow ivies.

refers to the first names, almost the surnames, of our garden shrubs. Every genus contains one or more species and all plants within the genus have basic characteristics in common. Well known examples of genera include *Cotoneaster*, *Forsythia*, *Hydrangea*, *Magnolia*, and *Potentilla*.

Species. Plants having more characteristics in common than the genera, occurring naturally and interbreeding freely, are known as species. Examples of well know *Cotoneaster* species are: *C. bullatus*, *C. dammeri*, *C. horizontalis*, *C. microphyllus*, *C. salicifolius*, *C. simonsii* and *C. sternianus*. All have an abundance of white or pink-tinged flowers loved by bees in early summer and attractive berries in autumn and winter.

Varieties. Species are variable in the wild, some to the point that they are distinct enough to be regarded separately as varieties. An example of this is *C. dammeri* var. *radicans*.

Cultivars. This term is normally used to describe plants which have arisen in cultivation usually as man-made hybrids, sports and chance seedlings. The term also embraces plants which have been specially selected in the wild for their distinctive shape form or colour and which are maintained in cultivation by vegetative propagation. The cultivar name is normally written in single quotation marks, for example 'Fructu-luteo', 'Parkteppich' and 'Repens'; all of these are cultivars of *Cotoneaster salicifolius*.

Clone. This is the term applied to a group of plants derived originally from a single unique specimen and increased by vegetative propagation. All plants of a single clone are exactly alike and identical to the original. It will be seen that most vegetatively propagated shrub cultivars are clonal. The term clonal is likely to be used more in the future now that modern scientific methods of eliminating virus diseases are being employed to

"clean up" old cultivars. Better growth has already been obtained from mother plants of *Prunus*, (flowering cherries) and *Malus* (flowering crabs), which have been free of viruses.

Hybrid. When a plant has been produced by the crossing of two genera or species, the Latin name is correctly preceded by a cross. For example, *Forsythia* x *intermedia* is the result of a cross between two *Forsythia* species, *F. suspensa* and *F. viridissima*.

There remains one further point of explanation: the change of plant names under the "Rule of Priority". It has been agreed that the earliest recorded name will be legitimate and with continuous historic research taking place many changes are made. One of the more recent changes that illustrates this point is the well known winter-flowering shrub *Viburnum fragrans*, now correctly known as *V. farreri*.

Cultivation

We are fortunate in that shrubs need so little routine cultural care. Unlike many border flowers, which may need dividing, replanting, their growing tips removed at special times, supporting, tying and so on, most shrubs continue to grow year after year, improving in appearance and giving more to the garden.

Even so it is worth giving them just a little extra care with regard to siting, soil, pruning and pest and disease control.

SOIL PREPARATION

Plants will cling desperately to life despite unsatisfactory conditions. It is worth remembering that, with just a little help, shrubs will not only live but flourish and grow with vigour. They will thrive in virtually all soils, the only qualification being to select carefully where extremes of alkalinity, acidity and bad drainage occur.

All perennial plants require a soil which has been well prepared by cultivation and manuring. If the

Tip
After planting shrubs, cover the surface with black polythene buried in soil at its edges to hold in place. Cover the polythene with chipped bark or similar material to improve the appearance. A few pin pricks should then be made to let water through. Given this treatment shrubs are maintenance-free, except for pruning, for twenty years or more.

Shrub growth will be lush and and free flowering given good planting conditions

SHRUBS FOR DIFFERENT SOILS

SANDY SOILS
Berberis
Cotoneaster
Cytisus
Elaeagnus
Hibiscus
Indigofera
Kerria
Ligustrum
Lonicera
Salix
Tamarix

CLAY SOILS
Abelia
Aralia
Aucuba
Berberis
Chaenomeles
Choisya
Cornus
Corylus
Cotinus
Cotoneaster
Deutzia
Escallonia
Forsythia
Hypericum
Mahonia
Osmanthus
Philadelphus
Potentilla
Pyracantha
Ribes
Rosa
Senecio
Spiraea
Symphoricarpos
Weigela

ACID SOILS
Acer
Azalea
Berberis
Calluna
Camellia
Cotoneaster
Erica
Hibiscus
Hydrangea
Indigofera
Kerria
Lonicera
Pernettya
Rhododendron
Tamarix

ALKALINE (Chalk) SOILS
Aucuba
Berberis
Buddleia
Buxus
Ceanothus
Cotoneaster
Deutzia
Euonymus
Forsythia
Fuchsia
Hebe
Hypericum
Laurus
Ligustrum
Olearia
Philadelphus
Potentilla
Rhus
Sambucus
Senecio
Symphoricarpos
Syringa
Weigela

preparation has been carried out thoroughly the life of the planting scheme will be lengthened.

Firstly, shrubs and plants with woody growth require at least 30cm of well-dug soil to accommodate the roots. Quick establishment and rapid growth will be achieved where there is ample depth of soil for free root growth.

All perennial weeds should be removed during the preparatory digging. Soils are greatly improved by the incorporation of well-rotted compost. Ideally therefore the soil should be cultivated to two spits, that is two spades' depth. This is most easily done by digging out a large hole one spit deep and then forking over the lower spit, digging in well-rotted garden compost and/or manure, or spent mushroom compost or similar organic planting composts at the same time

Adding organic matter improves the structure and texture of the soil and, contradictorily, both helps to hold moisture in the summer and allows free drainage in the winter. On very heavy clay soils the addition of coarse grit will also improve drainage.

Be careful to avoid preparing small round planting holes in heavy, poor soils such as are found on new building sites. These are apt to form drainage sumps which fill with water through the winter. In these conditions there is nothing to beat cultivating the whole area down to two spits deep during the autumn and then planting after it has settled in early spring.

Where double digging the whole site is out of the question, for most practical purposes digging over the top spit will suffice. If you come across a compacted area, do fork up the bottom of the trench as you dig across the plot.

It is advisable to spend at least as much on soil-improving organic material as you do on shrubs when planting in new gardens and poor soils. On heavy clay, for example, a 10–15cm layer of sphagnum peat thoroughly mixed into the soil will dramatically improve things. Not only will the roots and plants grow better but surface hoeing to control weeds will be so much easier.

Plant food in the form of fertilisers is easily applied after planting. The traditionally recommended dose of bone meal does encourage early root development but is an expensive source of plant food.

You will get better value for money by applying a good rose fertiliser at the recommended rates every spring. Ideally, also give a top-up in mid to late summer, if the conditions are moist enough to get it down to the roots. Well-fed plants are better able to withstand winter cold.

Where there are deep-rooted weeds in the soil it is advisable to treat their green leaves with glyphosate-based weedkillers a few weeks before digging. This weedkiller is taken down in the plant sap and kills the whole plant.

PLANTING

After cultivation, the site is best left for a period to settle before planting shrubs. Where it is necessary to plant into newly dug soil, firming by trampling may well be necessary after digging.

Should the shrub border be surrounded or edged by lawns, a planting sheet or board must be put down first on the turf. Spare soil from the planting hole can then be placed on the sheet until needed for refilling. Once the planting is complete the sheet is lifted to leave the grass unharmed and unsoiled.

A hole large enough to fully accommodate the shrub roots is needed. Always keep the bare roots of shrubs lifted from the soil protected from cold and drying winds by covering with damp sacking or cloth temporarily and, for longer periods, enclosing in damp sand, peat or soil.

Once the shrub is in the planting hole, good friable soil is filled in around the roots. Bare root shrubs should be eased up and down gently at the start of infilling to ensure the soil comes into close contact with the roots and that no large air pockets remain.

The soil is firmed by treading as the filling-in progresses. Once this is complete the footprints should be forked out. Where footprints are left to remain after planting the structure of the soil will be damaged by becoming wet and sticky after rain and then drying into a hard cake.

Soil structure, that lovely, easy-to-work, crumbly nature of earth in good heart, is also damaged by planting during wet conditions. When the soil

Tip

A few weed seedlings and mossy growth on the top of the compost along with signs of young root tips through the base of the pot are good indications of a fully container grown plants.

Before planting, water all container plants well. If the compost has dried out, it may be necessary to stand it in a saucer of water for half an hour or so to thoroughly rewet.

is very wet planting is better delayed, especially on heavy clay. Planting should also be postponed when the ground is frozen.

Well-grown container plants are the easiest to handle because in well-prepared soil we only need a hole fractionally larger than the container. Make sure that the plant is established in the container before purchasing. A few roots growing from the base and a little algae growth on

Make sure the shrubs has been container grown, freshly potted plants will need more care and are best treated like bare root plants. If grown in the container the roots will run through the compost.

Dig a hole and place the container grown plant in it to measure the depth. The hole should be slightly deeper than the pot such that after planting, a little fresh soil just covers the surface.

Remove the container; scratch off any weeds or moss from the surface into the base of the planting hole and check the roots around the bottom of the pot. If they have started to encircle it, carefully unravel some of them.

Once in place the soil, improved by the addition of more damp peat, is filled in around the roots. Firm the soil as you go, treading it down with your foot to ensure the new soil is in close contact with the old.

the top indicate well-established plants. They can also be carefully lifted by the stem and will hold the full weight of pot and compost.

Compost on the surface of recently potted plants will crack when lifted a little and they are best left with the nursery or garden centre until fully established.

Once the hole has been made, place the plant in position to check the depth. If right, the surface soil will be fractionally higher than the surface of the compost in the container. Remove the container and check the roots – if circling the base, tease the circle out a little. Fill in with fine soil and firm as you go. It is acceptable to leave the sacking-like material around balled plants if it will rot. man-made rotproof wrappings must be fully removed.

The compost in containers and soil contained in root-balled plants must be really moist before planting. Where the garden soil is less than wet,

especially from April to October, water plants well after planting and continue to water every week or so until established.

Where plants are bought or delivered in bad weather they will come to no harm, given the right treatment. Container plants just need watering to prevent the compost drying out.

Bare root plants should be left in the wrapping, free from frost and kept damp. When such plants arrive prior to site preparation they can be temporarily "laid-in", that is unwrapped and the roots placed in a trench on vacant ground, covered with moist soil and firmed.

PRUNING

Most shrubs grow and flower well for years with very little, if any, pruning. When gardening on a large scale this may be no more than retaining plant shape and proportion, where sensible removing dead flower heads and if

possible prune out a few old branches to rejuvenate growth. Small gardens need to be more productive, with every inch of space well used so regular pruning of many shrubs featured in this book is advisable. Where shrubs are established in well cultivated soils, pruning will prompt strong new growth, lush foliage and

Tip

It is easier to prune off thicker branches if, when the cut is made, pressure is applied downwards and away from the secateur blade, on the piece of shrub to be removed. Do not, however, press so hard the remaining branch splits.

Where shrubs are very over-grown and need drastic pruning to renew them cut out one-third of the old branches each year. This will ensure some flowers every year even if the new growth takes two years to reach the flowering stage.

Where cold causes die back in the winter prune out dead wood in spring

A light shearing over heathers as flowers fade keeps plant shape bushy

bigger flowers and fruits.

Remember the good general rule – the harder you prune the stronger healthy plants are likely to grow. There are of course exceptions to every rule so take note of the specific pruning instructions for each genera.

Be sure to have a good sharp pair of secateurs, both for the sake of the plant and for your your own comfort. Where stems are more than thumb thickness a small folding pocket pruning saw will make life a lot easier. When removing branches try to cut them out completely to avoid leaving a thicket of ugly stumps at the base of the shrub.

Pruning Evergreen Shrubs

Recently transplanted specimens which have had considerable root disturbance and reduction will need lead shoots – the strongest-growing branches – to be cut back by one half. Balled and container-grown plant require no more than the removal of weak, straggle and diseased pieces. Evergreens pruned in early spring quickly produce new growth to hide any unsightly cut ends. A few evergreens such as *Buxus*, *Lavandula* (young plants), *Mahonia*, *Olearia*,

Rhododendron, *Camellia* and *Santolina* (young plants) respond well to hard pruning. Where they are bare at the base or have outgrown their site, they can be pruned back in spring.

Pruning Deciduous Shrubs

– Late winter and spring-flowering shrubs, including such popular kinds as winter-flowering jasmine, *Forsythia*, flowering currants, lilac and *Weigela* are pruned hard immediately after flowering. This encourages strong new shoots which will flower well the next year.

– Early summer-flowering shrubs, such as *Deutzia*, *Escallonia*, *Hypericum*, *Philadelphus* and shrub roses require less harsh treatment. Thinning out a few of the older branches on well established plants after flowering is all they require.

– Late summer-flowering shrubs including *Buddleia davidii*, *Caryopteris*, hardy *Fuchsia*, *Clematis* x *jackmanii*, those Spiraeas grown for colourful new shoots and dogwoods grown for their colourful bark should have all stems cut hard back every year in early spring.

– Winter-flowering shrubs usually need little more than the removal of

weak non-productive branches and any dead wood in early spring. Where shrubs such as the winter-flowering Mahonias have become palm-tree-like they can be cut right down after flowering.

PESTS AND DISEASES

Fortunately this subject is a minor one when it comes to shrubs in gardens. Usually we have such a wide range of shrubs of different genera in our gardens there is no concentration of any one kind to magnify any one pest or disease.

Clean plants purchased or propagated at the outset, then grown well is the best way to stay free of problems. Buying cheap, poor-grade plants from rough, untidy growing conditions is foolish, to say the least.

There are a few general problems listed below along with some methods of control.

Aphids – greenfly, etc. Black sooty mould growing on the sticky honeydew exuded by aphids and the small white flecks of their cast-off skins are often the first symptoms of attack. By this stage the population will be quite high and insecticidal sprays will be needed. Commonly seen on beech hedges, berberis, honeysuckle, plums and apples. Deciduous plants can be sprayed with tar oil in winter to kill eggs and in summer with pirimicarb (Rapid) or similar greenly killer.

Caterpillars – a range of different caterpillars will eat shrub leaves but they are seldom in sufficient numbers to be a real problem. Where, for example on birch, they do defoliate young plants any caterpillar spray will give quick control.

Leaf miner – off-white tunnels in the leaves of plants as varied as holly, lilac and laburnum are caused by leaf miner larvae. Either pick off infected leaves and destroy them or kill the larvae at the tunnel end with a thumbnail, or spray with systemic insecticide at first sign of attack.

Scale – white, yellow or brown scales on the bark and down the veins on the undersides of leaves are sure signs of this pest. Heavy infestations will also encourage black sooty moulds. Spray deciduous shrubs with tar oil in winter, use either insecticides based on pyrethroids to kill the young crawlers in late spring/early summer or spray with systemic insecticide such as formothion in the growing season.

Vine weevil – one of our most serious garden pests, the adult eats notches out of leaf edges in late summer/early autumn. Each weevil lays hundreds of eggs at this time. However, the larvae do the real damage by eating the roots off many plants, especially *azalea*,

camellia, *rhododendron* and *hydrangea*. Watering the soil with a nematode parasite when temperatures are warm is one method of control. This is most effective for plants in pots and especially those in greenhouses and conservatories. A chemical based on imidachloprid, used as a soil insecticide and in composts by commercial growers, holds out our best chance of killing the larvae.

Clematis wilt – large-flowered clematis collapsing and dying as they come up to flower are the distressing symptoms of this disease. Avoid damaging the stem at soil level and water around the base of plants with systemic fungicide in spring to prevent attack. Spraying the base of large flowered clematis in May, when first spraying roses, with systemic fungicide is an easy way to remember this treatment.

Fireblight – affects pears, *pyracantha*, hawthorn and similar rosaceae shrubs. Leaves on branch tips look to have been blackened by fire and the bark exudes resinous sap. Affected plants are best removed and burnt.

Mildew – greyish felty growth on leaves usually caused by dryness at the root. Fungicide sprays, after a good watering, will usually clean up the problem.

Phytophthora – sudden death of *erica*, *camellia* and other ericaceous evergreens in hot summer weather is likely to be caused by this disease. It is soil-borne and worse in wet conditions. Dig out and destroy affected plants and replant

Powdery mildew

with other flowering plants not affected by this problem.

Rust – orange powdery spots on the undersides of leaves, this disease is controlled by spraying with Tumblite fungicide.

Virus – mottling of the leaves can be caused by aphis-carried virus diseases, especially on *Abutilon*. Control aphids to reduce the chances of those diseases.

Tip

Walk around the garden once a week from late spring to early autumn with a small sprayer filled with combined insecticide and fungicide. The very first sign of any pest or disease attack can then be dealt with and the need for extensive spraying to control severe attacks is considerably reduced.

Sooty mould

Fireblight

Vine weevil and vine weevil damage

Shrubs and Their Flowering Months

	Deciduous	Some Deciduous	Evergreen	Some Evergreen	White Flowers	Yellow Flowers	Orange Flowers	Red Flowers	Pink Flowers	Mauve Flowers	Blue Flowers	Nicely Fragrant	Jan	Feb	Mar	Apr	May	Jun	Jul	Aug	Sep	Oct	Nov	Dec
Abelia		🍃		🍃	✿														█	█	█			
Abutilon *megapotamicum*	🍃					✿		★											█	█				
Abutilon *vitifolium*	🍃				✿					✿							█	█						
Amelanchier	🍃				✿											█								
Arbutus			🍃		✿																	█	█	
Azalea		🍃		🍃	✿	✿	★	★	★	★		✓				█	█							
Berberis		🍃		🍃		✿	★									█	█							
Buddleja	🍃				✿		★	★	★	★									█	█	█			
Callistemon			🍃					★											█	█				
Camellia			🍃		✿			★	★					█	█	█								
Camellia *sasanqua*			🍃		✿			★	★			✓										█		
Carpenteria			🍃		✿														█					
Caryopteris	🍃										★									█	█			
Ceanothus			🍃								★						█							
Ceanothus	🍃									✿	★								█	█	█			
Cercis	🍃								✿							█	█							
Chaenomeles	🍃				✿		★	★	✿					█	█	█	█							
Chimonanthus	🍃					✿						✓	█	█										█
Choisya			🍃		✿							✓				█	█							
Cistus			🍃		✿			★	✿									█	█					
Clerodendrum	🍃				✿															█	█			
Convolvulus			🍃		✿													█	█	█				
Cornus *florida*	🍃				✿			★	✿								█							
Cornus *mas*	🍃					✿								█	█									
Corylopsis	🍃					✿						✓			█									
Cytisus	🍃				✿	✿	★	★								█	█							
Daphne	🍃								✿	✿		✓		█	█									
Deutzia	🍃				✿				✿									█						
Erica/Calluna			🍃		✿			★	✿	✿			█	█	█	█	█	█	█	█	█	█	█	█
Escallonia		🍃	🍃	🍃				★	✿										█	█				
Eucryphia			🍃		✿															█	█			
Exochorda	🍃				✿											█	█							
Fallopia	🍃				✿															█	█	█		
Fremontodendron			🍃			✿													█	█	█			

Shrubs and their Flowering Months

Shrub	Deciduous	Some Deciduous	Evergreen	Some Evergreen	White	Yellow	Orange	Red	Pink	Mauve	Blue	Fragrant	Jan	Feb	Mar	Apr	May	Jun	Jul	Aug	Sep	Oct	Nov	Dec
Forsythia	●					●									■									
Fuchsia	●				●			●	●										■	■	■			
Genista		●		●		●										■	■							
Hamamelis	●					●	●					✓	■	■										■
Hebe			●		●				●	●									■	■				
Hibiscus	●				●				●	●	●								■	■	■			
Hydrangea	●				●			●	●		●							■	■	■	■			
Hypericum		●		●		●													■	■				
Indigofera	●							●	●										■	■				
Jasminum *nud.*	●					●							■										■	■
Jasminum *off.*	●				●							✓							■	■				
Kalmia			●						●									■						
Kerria	●					●										■	■							
Kolkwitzia	●								●								■							
Laburnum	●					●											■							
Lavandula			●		●				●	●									■	■				
Lavatera	●				●				●	●									■	■	■			
Lonicera *x purpusii*	●					●						✓	■	■									■	■
Lonicera *periclymenum*	●					●						✓						■	■					
Magnolia	●				●				●						■	■								
Magnolia		●			●							✓						■	■					
Mahonia		●				●							■	■	■								■	
Malus	●				●			●	●							■	■							
Paeonia	●				●			●	●								■							
Perovskia	●										●									■	■			
Philadelphus	●				●							✓						■	■					
Pieris		●			●				●							■								
Potentilla	●				●	●	●		●									■	■	■				
Prunus	●				●				●						■	■							■	
Pyracantha		●			●													■						
Rhododendron		●			●			●	●	●						■	■							
Ribes	●				●			●	●						■	■								
Romneya	●				●							✓							■	■				
Rosa	●				●			●				✓						■	■					
Rosmarinus		●			●					●						■	■							
Rubus	●				●													■						
Salvia		●			●					●								■	■					
Sambucus	●				●													■						
Skimmia		●			●							✓				■								
Spartium	●					●												■	■					
Spiraea	●				●				●							■	■							
Syringa	●				●			●	●	●		✓					■	■						
Tamarix	●								●											■	■			
Viburnum *carlesii*	●				●							✓				■								
Viburnum *farreri*	●				●							✓	■										■	■
Viburnum *plicatum*	●				●												■	■						
Weigela	●							●	●								■	■						
Wisteria	●				●					●		✓					■	■						
Yucca			●		●														■	■				

SHRUBS FROM A–Z

Rhododendrons and azaleas, see pages 36 and 102

ABELIA

These summer and autumn flowering, deciduous, semi-evergreen and evergreen graceful shrubs deserve wider use. They flower for weeks, are easy to grow even in cold districts if given the protection of a south- or west-facing hedge or wall.

Throughout the flowering season many clusters of tubular flowers festoon the tips of branches and side-shoots. Attractive mid-to-dark green leaves are an excellent foil to the flowers and are attractive in their own right.

Abelia x grandiflora AGM is semi-evergreen, grows 1.5m in height and spread, the pink and white purplish-tinged flowers are slightly fragrant and produced from July to October. *A. x g.* 'Francis Mason' AGM from New Zealand has rich copper-coloured young growth which turns into yellowish-green leaves with darker centre, maturing to green but retaining a darker centre.

Abelia schumanii is slightly smaller with rosy-lilac bell-shaped flowers from June to September. It can get cut back by frost but like the rest of this *genera* shoots again from the ground in spring.

Abelia triflora grows to 3.5m and the white tinged-pink flowers have a heavenly scent. *Abelia* 'Edward Goucher' AGM is a small semi-evergreen shrub, free-flowering and ideal for the small garden.

Cultivation

Light loamy soils are best for *Abelia* but any open, free-draining soil is acceptable. Pruning is no more than the removal of old or dead wood after flowering. Propagate by taking half-ripe cuttings 8cm long in July and root in frames, ideally with some bottom heat. Generally pest and disease-free.

Abelia grandiflora 'Francis Mason'

Abutilon megapotamicum

ABUTILON

Soft-wooded shrubs, the Abutilons listed here need the shelter of a south or west wall in all but the warmest areas of Britain. *Abutilon megapotamicum* AGM is a very free-flowering sprawling shrub, often listed among climbers. An excellent conservatory plant growing at least 2m in height and spread. *A.m.* 'Variegatum' has mottled yellow leaves and is less hardy than the species.

Abutilon vitifolium is a near-hardy shrub which can survive the winter in Britain, where it reaches 2–3m in height and spread. In a warm climate it will grow to 5–10m and the maple- or vine-like leaves are grey-green and covered with greyish hairs on the underside.

The mallow-like flowers, mauve or lavender and 7cm across, form from May to October. *A.v. alba* has large white flowers and the somewhat hardier *A. x suntense* has mid-blue to mauve flowers.

Cultivation

Any well-drained garden soil is suitable and full sun is best although they will grow in partial shade if protected and warm. Ideally plant in May and protect the base of each plant with dry leaves or straw in frosty weather.

Prune out frost-damaged and dead stems from outdoor plants in spring. *Abutilon vitifolium* is easy to raise from seed sown indoors during March or April. They root quite easily from cuttings taken as half-ripe in June to August to root under glass. Whitefly, mealybug and scale pests can be a problem in conservatories. Systemic insecticides and/or predators may be needed to control these.

ACER – Maples, Sycamore

ACER – Maples, Sycamore

Among the very popular Acers, commonly referred to as maples, are true shrubs in dwarf and slow-growing forms and several which can be classified as small trees and large shrubs.

All are quite hardy, deciduous and have attractive foliage but rather insignificant flowers. They are easy to grow with the exception that some of the Japanese types need shelter when the new shoots develop quickly in spring to protect them from quick thawing after spring frost and bruising cold winds.

The "Box Elders", *Acer negundo*, are native to North America and can be grown either as bushy shrubs or standard trees. Both foliage and bark are bright green and the tree form grows to 8m in height and 5–6m spread.

Smaller forms with variegated and coloured leaves include *Acer negundo* 'Variegatum' (syn. *A.n.* 'Argenteo-variegatum') with broad white margins to the leaves, *A.n.* 'Elegans' with bright yellow variegation and *A.n.* 'Flamingo' AGM whose shoots open light pink and then turn green with white and pinkish variegation.

Slower growing, especially in the early stages, is *A. pseudoplatanus* 'Brilliantissimum' AGM, one of the sycamores. A chance seedling, it was found in 1864 by Charles Kershaw of Brighouse, Yorkshire. Eye-catching shrimp-pink shoots develop in early spring, open to pale yellow and

Tip

The Japanese Maples are excellent pot and tub plants, however keep the compost in pots on the dry side overwinter for the first few years. Wet rather than cold rots the roots.

Acer palmatum 'Dissectum Atropurpureum'

eventually turn a rather dull green above and purple beneath. After 100 years the original tree was no more than 7m so you can see it is not fast-growing.

All these are propagated by grafting and only need pruning to

Acer palmatum 'Bloodgood'

establish a good framework in their first three or so years. You need to prune *A.n.* 'Flamingo' hard in winter to get strong new growth on a stooled shrub and the best pink colouring.

Much smaller is *Acer japonicum* 'Aureum' which eventually grows to 6m but will take many years to reach 2m in most gardens. The attractive leaves are almost round, have 7–10 lobes and are pale golden-yellow through spring and summer. They contrast with the red flowers and seeds but have a tendency to scorch, so plant in partial or dappled shade.

Acer japonicum 'Aconitifolium' AGM is much stronger growing to 3m and has deeply-lobed green leaves that turn deep crimson in the autumn. Most popular of all are the *Acer palmatum* forms, especially those with deeply-cut leaves and slow-growing rounded habit, which suits the small garden. Most commonly called Japanese Maples their changing leaf colour in autumn is quite startling and includes all shades of red, orange and yellow.

Some of the best plants for the garden are the cut leaved Dissectum group such as: A.p. 'Dissectum' and

Acer negundo 'Flamingo'

A.p. 'Dissectum Viride' with finely-cut green leaves and A.p. 'Dissectum Atropurpureum' with somewhat variable reddish-purple young leaves turning purplish green in summer and attractive shades in autumn. A.p. 'Garnet' AGM is stronger growing with more coarsely cut leaves.

Not so deeply cut but equally good garden plants are A.p. 'Burgundy Lace' AGM with wine-red young leaves, A.p. 'Bloodgood' AGM reddish-purple all summer, A.p. 'Chitoseyama' AGM with an elegant, beautifully layered branch framework and A.p. 'Osakazuki' AGM with green leaves turning fiery red in autumn.

Among many other attractive cultivars A. p. 'Senkaki' is recommended for its coral pink bark – it is commonly called the "Coral Bark Maple". The variegated kinds with white- and pink-tipped leaves tend to scorch in strong sunlight.

Acer negundo 'Variegatum'

Cultivation

Acers are lime tolerant but grow best in moist, well-drained soil. Scale pests can spread along undersides of branches so spray with tar oil in winter or systemic insecticide in summer to control them. Sycamores get sooty mould following aphid attack, spray as for scale to prevent this problem.

Propagation is by grafting onto seedling rootstocks, layering and softwood cuttings, all of which are skilled operations. While they do not come true from seed, sown just before it is fully ripe seed germinates fairly easily outside and in cold frames.

Acer palmatum 'Osakazuki'

ACTINIDIA

There are two vigorous-growing deciduous climbing Actinidias for gardens. "Kiwi Fruit" or "Chinese Gooseberry", *Actinidia chinensis*, needs a warm wall and male and female varieties for pollination to fruit in Britain. More commonly planted, for the white- and pink-tipped leaves on older plants, is *Actinidia kolomikta*. This reaches 4–7m and is suitable for all walls including those facing north.

Cultivation

Actinidia kolomikta grows well in most garden soils and in sun or semi-shade. Prune in February if necessary to restrain or tidy the twining stems and propagate by half-ripe cuttings in July and August.

AMELANCHIER

Commonly called "Snowy Mespilus" and in Germany and Holland "Currant Tree" because they dried the fruit like currants, Amelanchiers make large shrubs or small trees. They are very attractive in spring when the young leaves are pink to copper, in rich contrast to the masses of starry white flowers. The leaves turn lovely shades of red and orange before they fall in autumn.Small scarlet rounded fruits turn purple, are sweet-tasting and loved by birds.

Amelanchier lamarckii AGM grows quite fast to 6m high and 2–3m wide. It also makes an attractive small tree on a single trunk suitable for a small garden. The size can be controlled by pruning after flowering.

Cultivation

Both open and shaded sites are suitable for *Amelanchier* and moist, slightly acid soils are best. They will grow happily in most garden soils, excepting shallow, dry chalk.

Actinidia kolomikta

Amelanchier lamarkii

ARBUTUS

Tall evergreen shrubs and small trees, *Arbutus* have small pitcher-shaped pink to white flowers in clusters from October to December and some have attractive bark. Fruits ripen twelve months after flowering, turn red and look like strawberries, hence the common name "Strawberry Tree".

Arbutus unedo 'Rubra' AGM has a more dwarf, bushy habit and is less common because it needs grafting. They do not transplant easily so always use pot-grown stock for garden planting.

AUCUBA

An excellent town plant, *Aucuba* withstands dense shade, the competition of tree roots and dirty city air. It is most attractive, however, when growing well in clean conditions, when the glossy leaves become an eye-catching feature. Variegated forms retain the best colour in sunny sites.

Male and female flowers appear on separate plants and with cross pollination the females produce bright scarlet berries. The first plant introduced from Japan in 1780 was *Aucuba japonica* 'Variegata', a yellow-spotted female form but no berries were seen in Britain until a male was introduced seventy years later.

Aucuba japonica has glossy dark green leaves, grows 1.5m in height and spread and is usually male. *A.j.* 'Longifolia' AGM has long, bright green leaves and *A.j.* 'Salicifolia' has even narrow leaves, both are female and berry freely if pollinated.

The common name "Spotted Laurel" indicates a number of brightly variegated leaf forms such as: *A.j.* 'Crotonifolia' AGM, large-leaved with bright green yellow speckling, male; *A.j.* 'Goldstrike', heavily splashed with golden spots, male; *A.j.*

Arbutus unedo

'Sulphurea', dark green foliage with yellow edge, female; *A.j.* 'Picturata', golden centre, green edge to leaves, male.

Useful evergreens for shrubberies, for containers, window boxes, even houseplants where something is needed to withstand low light and low temperatures.

Use a half-and-half mix of John Innes Potting Compost and all peat compost for container growing.

Flower arrangers will find these shrubs a useful source of evergreen and brightly coloured foliage when cut blooms are in short supply.

Cultivation

Most *Arbutus* prefer an acid soil although *Arbutus unedo* AGM is lime-tolerant, one of the few ericaceous plants with this quality.

No pruning save the removal of winter, frost-damaged shoots in April. Young plants are tender so protect them with fine mesh netting in very cold weather, filling in with dry leaves for extra insulation. Propagate from seed sown when fully ripe in March or from half-ripe cuttings in July.

Cultivation

All garden soils are suitable for *Aucuba* but the best leaf colour and berry size comes from well cultivated garden soils and some fertiliser each spring.

Little pruning is necessary although they respond when old or damaged stems are cut back in April.

Species are propagated by seeds, named cultivars from cuttings in August/September rooted in sandy soil in a cold frame.

Aucuba japonica 'Crotonifolia'

AZALEA

AZALEA

Botanically *Azalea* is now placed under the genera heading *Rhododendron*. In general garden terms, however, the two are usually considered separately. The taller kinds lose their leaves in autumn while the lower-growing kinds are virtually evergreen.

EVERGREEN AZALEAS

Many of the hybrids in this category produce two sets of leaves, those formed in spring falling in the autumn but the second flush of summer leaves lasting through the winter. In periods of hard frost some of the less hardy cultivars such as 'Kirin' (syn. 'Coral Bells') AGM with rich pink hose-in-hose (one trumpet flower in another) flowers will drop their leaves. They then flower quite attractively on leafless stems and soon produce new spring foliage.

The general name Japanese is often used to describe evergreen azaleas and many were bred in Kurume, a town in Japan, from *Rhododendron kaempferi* and other species. Good Kurume azaleas are: 'Addy Wery' AGM, deep vermilion overlaid orange; 'Hino-Crimson' AGM, deep crimson; 'Hino-Mayo' AGM, clear silver-pink on wide horizontal fan-shaped branches and 'Rosebud' AGM, a late-flowering deep pink hose-in-hose on a low spreading plant.

Dutch plant breeders raised many hybrids crossing *R. kaempferi* with *R.* 'Malvaticum' in the 1920s to give rise to the Kaempferi group, many of which have girls' names such as: 'Alice' salmon red; 'Betty' AGM salmon pink; 'Fedora' AGM, pale pink. Some large-flowered cultivars of this type were raised by Vuyk van Nes of Boskoop, Holland. The Vuyk hybrids include: 'BlueDanube' AGM; 'Palestrina' AGM, white with green throat; 'Vuyk's Rose Red' AGM; and 'Vuyk's Scarlet' AGM.

DECIDUOUS AZALEAS

There are four broad groups within the deciduous type, growing to 1.5–2.5m and a little taller in semi-shade and good growing conditions. The flowers are trumpet-shaped, mostly single, in colours ranging from soft pastel pink to brilliant orange and yellow and some are fragrant.

1. GHENT hybrids come from a cross between *Rhododendron luteum* from Eastern Europe (the yellow *Azalea ponticum* now found growing wild in Britain) and *R. calendulaceum*, brilliantly coloured yellow to orange and almost scarlet, like the calendula namesake, from North America. The first American plants are said to have arrived in Belgium by chance after a ship bound for France was blown off course and wrecked in Holland in

Azalea mollis

Japanese azaleas

1797. The wealthy French importer fell foul of the guillotine and his American azaleas were left in private gardens in Ghent.

Several other species are now bred into this group to give typically long, honeysuckle-tubed, fragrant flowers including: R. 'Coccineum Speciosum' AGM, orange-red; R. 'Nancy Waterer' AGM, golden yellow; and R. 'Narcissiflorum' AGM pale yellow and very sweetly scented.

2. KNAPHILL hybrids come from crosses between GHENT hybrids, *R. molle*, *R. occidentale* and several other species. They were made by Anthony Waterer of Knaphill, Surrey and his work was continued by Lionel Rothschild at Exbury. Good examples are: 'Cecile' AGM, salmon-pink with yellow flush; 'Debutante' pink with orange blotch; and 'Persil' AGM,

white with yellow flare.

3. EXBURY hybrids include 'Hotspur Red' AGM; 'Klondkye' AGM, deep gold and bronze leaves; and 'Strawberry Ice' AGM pink flushed orange.

4. MOLLIS azaleas come from *R. japonicum* x *R. molle* and there are good strains raised from seed which come pretty well true to colour. They have large flowers which open before the leaves and the salmon pinks look delightful above a carpet of forget-me-nots or bluebells.

Cultivation

All azaleas need an acid, peaty soil and grow best in partial shade. They grow very well in containers of ericaceous compost.

Be sure to keep container-grown plants well watered during the summer with lime-free water, ideally rainwater.

The removal of seed heads after flowering improves growth and the next year's flowering, an impractical task on sizeable japanese types but well worthwhile on larger-flowered kinds.

Azaleas respond well to hard pruning after flowering, if this should become necessary, to rejuvenate leggy plants.

The Japanese kinds root fairly easily from soft to half ripe cuttings in early summer, the rest are most easily propagated by layering lower branches.

Azalea gall is a disfiguring disease of evergreen types, producing red and pale green leaf swellings followed by white spores. Remove and burn galls and spray with bordeaux or a more modern fungicide. Vine weevil is a serious pest controlled by watering on nematode parasites in autumn.

Azalea 'Klondyke'

Azalea 'Nancy Waterer'

BAMBOO

BAMBOO

There are a number of shrubby plants which are members of the grass family, generally referred to as "Bamboos". They provide food, fuel, building materials, screens and decoration. While their dense growth and oriental appearance can be very useful they are not as widely grown in Britain as their qualities deserve.

One of the most widely listed, *Arundinaria murieliae* (syn. *Fargesia murieliae*) AGM is a strong-growing plant with elegant 2.5–3.5m high arching green canes which turn dull yellow with age. Ernest Wilson introduced this plant from China in 1913 and named it after his daughter. *A. nitida* (syn. *fargesia nitida*) AGM is very hardy, similar to *murieliae* but with purple canes which contrast with the narrower green leaves. It grows best in a little shade.

There are more than 50 species of *Phyllostachys* which have zig-zag-shaped stems and like moist soils. *P. aurea* AGM forms large clumps 2.5–3.5m tall with bright green canes turning dull yellow in full sun, while *P. nigra*, "Black Bamboo", has green canes that turn mottled brown/black in warm positions.

Pleioblastus is a genus of small to medium types with underground suckering stems, some being very invasive. Many now named *Pleioblastus* were previously classified under *Arundinaria*, for example one of the best variegated bamboos, *A. viridistriata* is now *Pleioblastus auricomus*, a

Phyllostachys nigra

good tub plant at only 1m or so high in shade. Old stems can be cut hard back in spring to get colourful young leaves. *P. humilis* – dark green leaves and slender canes 0.5–1.5m high and *P. pumila*, 0.3–0.6m with hairy joints up the stem, are invasive plants which provide good ground cover under trees.

Cultivation

Most are easy to grow in all soils including chalk, but avoid heavy, waterlogged clay. Cold northerly and easterly winds can brown the foliage. Under garden conditions many bamboos fail to flower but when they do some will die out after flowering. Propagation is by division in March to May. Do not let the roots get dry when dividing and after replanting until well established.

Pleioblastus humilis

BERBERIS

There is no better plant than *Berberis* to deter vandals, both two- and four-legged kinds. They are commonly called "Barberry", a name which comes from the Arabic, where we also find the Berber tribe and the anglicised Barbary Coast of the western part of North Africa once well known for pirates and slavery. Three sharp, long thorns at each leaf-joint characterise these evergreen and deciduous shrubs.

Among the hundred or more different species are cultivars which offer gardeners attractive foliage – some brilliantly coloured in the autumn – flowers and fruits. Several make impenetrable hedges and the coloured-leaved forms provide coveted shoots for floral arrangement.

EVERGREENS range from the compact *Berberis buxifolia* 'Nana', making neat mounds 60cm or so high to *B x stenophylla* AGM, a popular hedge plant reaching 3m if left uncut.

The latter produces a thicket of arching stems which form an impenetrable barrier that is covered in golden flowers in April and May.

One of the most popular of all garden plants is *B. darwinii* AGM, with small shiny dark green leaves providing an excellent foil to the yellow flushed crimson flowers and subsequent purple berries. This grows quite slowly, eventually reaching 2m in height and 1.5m spread, a size easily restrained by pruning. Outstanding flower colour is provided by *B. linearifolia* 'Orange King' with upright, rather thin growth and orange flowers that deepen to red and *B. x lologensis* 'Apricot Queen' AGM with masses of pale orange flowers, both in April.

An alternative for screening is *B. julianae* which reaches 3m and 1.2m spread, the dense growth carrying glossy green leaves that turn red in the autumn. Among a number of cultivars selected for their low-growing ground-covering form are *B.*

Berberis darwinii

x *frikartii* 'Amstelveen' AGM, with leaves glossy green above, bluish-white beneath and *B. x media* 'Parkjuweel' (Park Jewel) AGM that has very good autumn colour, often carried well into winter. One plant of both will cover one square metre or so of soil.

DECIDUOUS types are dominated by *Berberis thunbergii* AGM cultivars. These excellent garden plants which grow little more than 1.5m in height and spread, have flowers of pale yellow speckled with red in spring followed by bright red

Berberis x stenophylla

BERBERIS

fruits. The original species has green leaves that turn brilliant red before they fall in autumn.

Some of the cultivars have more eye-catching foliage colour, for example *B.t.* 'Atropurpurea' has dark bronze leaves in spring which pale to bronzy green in summer before turning vivid red. *B.t.* 'Atropurpurea Nana' AGM is a smaller edition growing slowly to 0.5m and *B.t.* 'Bagatelle' AGM is even more compact. An upright form producing a column of deep bronze leaves all summer is *B.t.* 'Helmond Pillar'.

Other leaf colours available include: *B.t.* 'Aurea' with bright yellow leaves which age to pale green, it can scorch in hot sun and grows better in damp conditions; *B.t.* 'Dart's Red Lady' which has a more spreading habit and very dark purple leaves; *B.t.* 'Harlequin' with pinkish leaves ageing to purple with white splashes; *B.t.* 'Red Chief' AGM is taller, to 1.8m with arching branches covered in red to purple leaves; and *B.t.* 'Rose Glow' AGM has silver pink and bright rose young leaves that turn purple in summer.

A large flamboyant hybrid from *B. thunbergii* crossed with British native *B. vulgaris* is B. x *ottawensis* 'Superba' growing to 2m and more in height with elegant branches lined with oval leaves of richest purple. Less dramatic in summer but also colourful in autumn is *B. wilsoniae* growing to 1m with deep yellow flowers followed by jade green fruits that ripen to coral red.

Tip
The long prickly stems pruned from, for example, B. x *ottawensis* 'Superba' are useful spaced over newly sown and freshly cultivated soil to deter cats and other animals.

Berberis thunbergii 'Rose Glow'

Berberis thunbergii 'Atropurpurea Nana'

Berberis thunbergii 'Aurea'

Berberis thunbergii 'Red Chief'

Cultivation

All garden soils, including chalky ones, are suitable and the evergreens tolerate some shade, as do some of the more exotic-coloured *B. thunbergii* cultivars. Transplant deciduous types between October and March and evergreens in September and October or in March and April. Avoid transplanting losses by purchasing container-grown plants.

Berberis require little pruning save the removal of old unwanted branches in spring. The coloured-leaved kinds produce the best colour on the young shoots so don't be afraid to thin out some old growth on mature plants each spring. New shoots soon sprout from below big cuts, which expose the bright yellow wood. Evergreens can be trimmed either after flowering or in August.

Species are easily raised from seed sown in the open in late autumn but crosses are likely to produce wide variety in the seedlings. Most are propagated from side shoots of the current year's growth 7.5–10cm long pulled off with a heel of older bark in August/September. Placed in peat and sand in a cold frame, they should be rooted by the following spring.

A few cultivars such as *B.l.* 'Orange King' are grafted, so a watch should be kept for suckers which when seen should be cut cleanly away.

Sprays may be needed in spring and early summer to kill aphids which if left cause a black sticky mould to develop to disfigure the leaves.

BUDDLEIA

Butterflies are attracted to *Buddleia* as if by magnetism, to the point that the plant has been called the "Butterfly Bush". For this reason alone *Buddleias* are worthy of a place in every garden. Their fragrant flowers can provide colour from May to September, using a selection of species.

The first to flower is *Buddleia alternifolia* AGM which grows into a large shrub or small tree 3m or so in height and spread. The arching sprays of fragrant lilac flowers are produced in June.

Reginald Farrer, who introduced the plant to Britain, described it as a 'gracious small-leaved weeping willow, when it is not in flower, and a sheer waterfall of soft purple when it is'. The leaves differ from other species in being alternate up the stem, hence the name.

Buddleias were named after the Rev. Adam Buddle, an Essex vicar and the plant was first found by

Buddleia alternifolia

another religious man, the French missionary Monsieur David, in 1889. However the first plants to arrive in Britain came from Russia – poor things with loose, ungainly habit and pale-coloured flowers. A better form came from France in 1893 but it was the great plant collector Ernest Wilson who introduced the ancestors of our modern day hybrids between 1900 and 1908.

Cultivars of *Buddleia davidii* are by far the most widely planted. They never fail to produce an abundance of showy flower spikes from July throughout the summer. Popular plants! Examples include: *B.d.* 'Black Knight' AGM, deep purple; *B.d.* 'Charming', lavender pink; *B.d.* 'Empire Blue' AGM; and *B.d.* 'Royal Red' AGM. *Buddleia globosa* AGM provides a complete contrast with its globular, tangerine-orange flowers. Commonly called the "Orange Ball Tree", it is virtually evergreen, the leaves falling only in severe weather. It flowers in June and grows to 2.5–3m in height and spread.

Smaller growing to 1.5m and very free-flowering are *B.d.* 'Nanho Blue' and *B.d.* 'Nanho Purple', both excellent small garden plants flowering for two months or more if dead flower heads are cut off. *Buddleia lindleyana* 'Lochinch' AGM has silver-grey young leaves, an excellent background to the pale mauve flowers with orange eye.

Less common with orange-yellow, flushed lilac flowers through the summer is *B. x weyeriana* 'Golden Glow' and its deep orange sport *B. x w.* 'Sungold' AGM 2–3m.

Tip

The long stems pruned from *Buddleia davidii* make useful cane substitutes to support smaller plants.

Buddleia davidii

Buddleia globosa

Cultivation

Any well cultivated garden soil is suitable and a sunny site is preferred. The way self-sown seedlings grow in rubble and old walls indicates their tolerance of lime and ability to survive in light, well drained soils. Strong-growing *B. globosa* merely needs trimming to shape after flowering. *B. alternifolia* can be restrained and kept neat and bushy by pruning back two thirds of flowering stems after flowering. *B. davidii* cultivars respond well to hard pruning back to 5–7.5cm from old wood in early March. It is as well to allow plants to establish for two years, especially the 'Nanho' cultivars, before hard pruning annually.

Buddleias are easily propagated by half-ripe non-flowering side-shoots 10–12.5cm long taken in July and August and rooted in sandy compost. *B. davidii* can also be rooted from hardwood cuttings of current season's growth 30cm long taken in October and rooted in sandy soil.

Buddleia davidii 'Black Knight'

Buddleia davidii 'Nanho Blue'

Buddleia davidii 'Royal Red'

BUXUS

Buxus, commonly called "Box" in Britain and "Boxwood" in the States, is best known as either a neatly trimmed topiary specimen or in its dwarf form as neat edging to Victorian-style vegetable gardens and low hedges in knot gardens.

Buxus sempervirens AGM is a native British evergreen eventually forming a small tree 10m high, while *B.s.* 'Suffruticose' AGM is the dwarf form, growing to 30cm or so. There are numerous garden cultivars with slightly different plant habit, leaf shape and colour.

Members of the Box Society of America grow over 70 different garden forms. These include: *B.s.* 'Aurea Pendula' which makes a 3m shrub of rather loose habit with leaves striped and mottled yellow; *B.s.* 'Elegantissima' AGM is the best silver box, slow-growing and with leaves marked creamy-white; *B.s.* 'Gold Tip' (syn. *B.s.* 'Notata') has deep green leaves, the upper ones on lead shoots edged yellow; *B.s.* 'Pyramidalis' has rich dark green leaves and an upright habit; *B.s.* 'Rotundifolia' is a smaller form with neat rounded leaves.

Buxus in a container

All have the typical, rather strange, box scent which is especially strong on warm sunny days and when leaves are crushed. Branches last for weeks when cut and placed in water. Short pieces are the ideal infill for table decorations of cut flowers.

Tip

A metre row of cuttings should provide enough plants for 3m of low box hedging.

Topiary

Cultivation

Buxus is easy to grow, thriving in sun and shade and all garden soils are suitable, including chalk. Transplanting from the open soil is best done in September/October and March/April while pot grown stock can be planted year round.

Old low hedges can be rejuvenated by lifting, dividing and planting by burying half to two thirds of the stem at a $45^{\emptyset}$ angle back into deeply dug soil.

Propagation is by 7.5cm cuttings put in sandy soil in August, by division of bushy plants in October or March and by layering in September/October.

Prune and trim in May, July and August/September. The earlier trimming allows new growth to cover and hide the cut ends. Use the later dates for once a year trimming.

Small white suckers sometimes feed on the leaves and cause distortion, control with insecticides such as malathion.

Buxus – hedging

CALLICARPA

Quite remarkable berries are the feature of *Callicarpa bodinieri* var. *giraldii*. The rather insignificant lilac flowers are followed by dense clusters of bright lilac-to-purple fruits, like small evenly coloured pearls, from September to Christmas. Biggest berry size is seen in its native North America in acid soil and warm summer temperatures. *C.b.* var. 'Profusion' AGM is very free fruiting and has bronze-coloured young growth.

Tip

Grow plants in large pots and tubs to bring into unheated conservatories to fully appreciate their autumn leaf and bright berry colour.

The berries provide an unusual colour for modern flower arrangements.

Cultivation

Callicarpa reaches 2m and is best in mixed shrubberies where it will receive some shelter from hard frost. Dry leaves around the base will give protection in hard frost and where branch damage does occur they soon re-shoot from the base in spring.

Pruning is no more than taking out old branches to retain shape in spring. Propagate from cuttings taken with a heel of old growth in June or July. Root these in peat and sand in the warm and keep under glass through the first winter. They are generally pest and disease-free.

CALLISTEMON

The common name "Bottle-brush" accurately describes *Callistemon*, an unusual flowering shrub from Australia and Tasmania. The flowers form on the tips of branches which then grow on, extending the stem and trapping the seed capsules for years.

Callistemon citrinus is the most common species with typical narrow green leaves which smell of lemon when crushed and dense spikes of red flowers in summer. *C.c.* 'Splendens' AGM has brilliant scarlet flowers.

Cultivation

Callistemon is a plant for warm, sheltered gardens and in many parts of Britain better grown in pots and tubs in conservatories. All well-drained garden soils are suitable except chalk.

Callistemon needs little pruning and is generally pest and disease-free. Propagation is by seed and half-ripe cuttings made from sideshoots from June to August and rooted in peat and sand in the warm.

CALLUNA – see Heathers

Callistemon citrinus

Callicarpa bodnieri var. 'Profusion'

CAMELLIA

CAMELLIA

Most of the species and cultivars listed here are quite hardy and under favourable conditions will grow to at least 2m high and 1–2m across. All types have handsome glossy evergreen leaves that are attractive enough to recommend planting more.

The flower forms include; singles with one row of not more than eight petals around a cluster of yellow stamens; semi-doubles with two or more rows of petals; anemone-centred with one or more rows of large petals surrounding a semi-globular mass of intermingled smaller petals and stamens; paeony-flowered with a mass of petals of all shapes in double paeony form; double with several rows of overlapping petals in open saucer shape around yellow stamens; and formal double with fully overlapping petals so complete there are no stamens. The flower sizes vary from very large – over 12.5cm across, down to small – 5–7.5cm.

There are four main species of interest to gardeners: *Camellia japonica*, the common *camellia* is a large evergreen shrub available in thousands of different cultivars. Good examples include *C.j.* 'Alba Plena', a white large formal double; *C.j.* 'Noblissima', white to cream paeony (early flowering – December to February – so can be damaged by frost); *C.j.* 'Debutante', light pink medium-sized flowers on an upright plant; *C.j.* 'Mathotiana Rosea' a large formal double (the white form, *C.j.* 'Mathotiana Alba' AGM is more tender and not recommended for cold positions); *C.j.* 'Nagasaki' rose-pink mottled white large semi-double, leaves often marked yellow, branches having a spreading habit; *C.j.* 'Adolphe Audusson' AGM semi-double blood red with contrasting yellow stamens, good grower and well-tried plant; *C.j.* 'Mercury' AGM bright red semi-double; and *C.j.* 'R.L. Wheeler' AGM rose-pink semi-double-to-anemone.

Camellia reticulata, the true species, grows into a large compact shrub up to 10m in warm situations. Its dull net-veined green leaves are an excellent foil to the rose pink flowers from late winter through early spring. The flowers are somewhat trumpet-shaped when fully out. *C.r.* 'Captain Rawes' AGM is a large semi-double deep rose pink.

Camellia sasanqua is a winter and very early spring flowering species producing small fragrant flowers. Best given the protection of a south wall, especially as young plants although it flowers well outside on a north slope in Wisley Gardens, Surrey. A good conservatory plant. *C.s.* 'Crimson

Camellia sasanqua

You are unlikely to see Chinese women wearing camellia flowers because the many months it takes the flower buds to open are equated with the long wait for a son. Japanese Samurai warriors, on the other hand, see them as symbols of war-like spirit, of fair play and purpose, because the bright red double flowers eventually fall as if beheaded! This is the reason camellia flowers frequently feature in decorations on their swords and other weapons.

CAMELLIA

Cultivation

Camellia are excellent as single specimens best grown against a west or north-facing wall. They can be grown mixed in shrub borders, in partial shade under trees and, best of all, as tub and container plants. In northern gardens and too-shady places flowering is reduced but everywhere it is better to avoid scorching hot dry positions in full sun.

Ideally, site plants so they are sheltered from strong winds and shaded from early morning sun which causes rapid thawing after frost and browning of the petals. They all dislike chalk and lime. Alkaline soils as in Guernsey cause a yellowing of the leaves. Watering in April with sequestrene, mulching with peat and adding flowers of sulphur to the soil can all help to correct this.

Most plants are gown in peat and bark composts which, once very dry, are difficult to re-wet. If left dry camellias drop their flower buds.

When over-large, camellias respond well to hard pruning, best done after flowering and before the surge of new growth.

They are propagated by half-ripe cuttings 7.5–10cm long, ideally with a heel, taken June to August. Vine weevil, aphids, mealy bugs and scale are all likely pests under glass especially. There are biological and insecticidal controls for all these problems.

Camellia j. 'Adolfe Audusson'

King' AGM, bright red single flowers with yellow stamens, is often in flower at Christmas.

Ancient trading bans delayed *C. sasanqua* leaving China where it provided oil and an inferior grade of tea – *sasanqua* is said to come from Japanese *sazankwa*, a plum-flavoured tea. This plant responds well to trimming and training and modern cultivars are being used in hanging baskets.

Camellia x *williamsii* make the best garden plants and come from crosses between *C. japonica* and *C. saluenensis*. They have proved hardy, easy to grow and early to come into flower. Raised first by Mr J.C. Williams at Caerhays Castle, Cornwall, who introduced the excellent medium-sized single pink *C.* x *w.* 'J.C. Williams' AGM and later by Col. Stephenson Clark in Sussex who raised one of the most successful of all in *C.* x *w.* 'Donation' AGM, a large semi-double pink with strong upright growth. Other good cultivars are *C.* x *w.* 'Anticipation' AGM, large deep rose anemone form; *C.* x *w.* 'Brigadoon' AGM, hardy large semi-double pink; *C.* x *w.* 'Elsie Jury' AGM, large pink anemone-flowered; and *C.* x *w.* 'St Ewe' AGM medium single bell-shaped rose pink.

Camellia 'Cornish Snow' AGM is worthy of mention being early and long-flowering in the garden. Smaller, narrower leaves are produced on a loose open shrub and the small single white flowers are trumpet-shaped and have yellow stamens.

Camellia x williamsii 'Donation'

Camellia x williamsii 'Debbie'

Camellia

47

CARPENTERIA

CARPENTERIA

Akin to *Philadelphus* and a native of California, *Carpenteria californica* AGM is an evergreen, reasonably hardy but best planted with the protection of a south-facing wall or fence. It can reach 6m but 2–3m in height and spread is more usual.

Carpenteria californica

Cultivation

Most garden soils are acceptable for *Carpenteria* as long as they are well drained. This shrub flowers best in poor, stony soils and hot sun. The species produces clusters of 3–7 flowers in June–July and *Carpenteria californica* 'Ladham's Variety' has larger flowers up to 8cm across.

Regular pruning is not required and any re-shaping is done after flowering. Old stems cut to the ground will soon be replaced.

Propagation is by seed sown March/April or by layering the larger and freer-flowering forms.

They are generally pest- and disease-free.

CARYOPTERIS

The "Blue Spiraea", *Caryopteris* x *clandonensis* with its greyish-green aromatic leaves is a useful garden plant. Masses of bright blue flowers are produced on low arching branches from August to October. It grows to little more than 1m in height and spread and can be used to the front of shrub borders and among herbaceous plants.

Mr Arthur Simmonds, former Secretary of The Royal Horticultural Society, raised the specific hybrid and there are several good cultivars. *Caryopteris* x *c.* 'Arthur Simmonds' is bright blue; *C.* x *c.* 'Ferndown' has

Tip

Prunings from *Caryopteris* make useful supports for hardy annuals and such pot plants as freesias, schizanthus and Reiger begonias.

Cultivation

Caryopteris thrive in virtually every soil type, especially chalk and are best suited to full sun and well-drained positions.

All cultivars are best pruned back hard every February or March when the previous year's growth is cut back to 5cm from the old wood.

Propagate by taking cuttings 7.5–10cm long of half-ripe shoots in August/September and root in peat and sand in a cold frame. They are generally pest- and disease-free.

slightly darker blue-violet flowers and *C.* x *c.* 'Heavenly Blue' AGM is a little more compact and slightly deeper in colour than 'Arthur Simmonds'. *C.* x *c.* 'Worcester Gold' has golden foliage and bright blue flowers.

Caryopteris x *clandonensis* 'Heavenly Blue'

CEANOTHUS

Blue is a somewhat elusive colour in the garden and *Ceanothus* provides it. Commonly called "Californian Lilac" after its native state where they can be seen flowering in great masses half way up the mountain ranges in shrubby cover called "chaparral".

Easily grouped into evergreens, with somewhat smaller, cleaner, rich dark green leaves, most of them early to midsummer flowering and the deciduous types with larger pale green leaves and late summer to early autumn flowering.

Evergreens:

Ceanothus 'A.T. Johnson' grows vigorously to 3m with rich blue flowers in May/June and again in the autumn; C. 'Blue Mound' AGM is free flowering, deep blue reaching

Ceanothus 'Gloire de Versailles'

Ceanothus 'Blue Mound'

1.5m height and 3m spread, C. *dentatus* has tiny leaves and bright blue May flowers; C. *prostratus* 'Puget Blue' AGM has deeply impressed veins to the small leaves and deep lilac May flowers, is upright and will reach 2m in three years or so against a wall; C. *thyrsiflorus repens* AGM "Creeping Blue Blossom", one of the hardiest, covers the ground in a low mound 1m high and 2.5m across.

Deciduous in cold winters:

Ceanothus 'Gloire de Versailles' has clusters 20–30cm long of tiny light blue flowers from July to October on branches reaching 2–3m high; C. 'Marie Simon', rose pink; and C, 'Topaze' AGM indigo-blue flowers.

Cultivation

Ceanothus are good free-standing and wall shrubs which require a warm site, full sun and free-draining soil. Coastal conditions suit them and acid to alkaline conditions. Cold winters will cause some of the evergreens to drop their leaves and where frost kills back branches, saw off the damaged wood in April. Older, very woody plants can be killed right back by frost and are less likely than younger ones to shoot out again.

Evergreens can be pruned after flowering, especially the sideshoots on branches trained horizontally against walls. Deciduous types should be allowed to produce several stout branches 0.6m high in the first two or three years. Then prune back the previous year's flowered wood in March. Take half-ripe cuttings with a heel in July and keep these protected through the winter before potting up in spring. Should scale insects attack the undersides of leaves spray with systemic insecticide. Leaves may yellow in chalky soil, indicating a need for iron.

CERCIS

CERCIS

According to legend Judas Iscariot hanged himself on *Cercis siliquastrum*, hence the common name "Judas Tree": an unlikely story bearing in mind the brittle branches. The French common name "Judea Tree" at least tells its origins.

A slow-growing tree or large shrub, it has deep pink pea-shaped flowers growing in clusters from old wood, even straight from the trunk, in May. There is a white-flowered form not freely available.

Cultivation

Cercis requires light, free-draining soil and full sun. Its fleshy roots do not take kindly to transplanting. Propagation is by seed sown under glass in March. They require no pruning save the complete removal and burning of branches infested with coral spot disease.

CHAENOMELES

Outstanding garden plants, the *Chaenomeles* is known by such common names as "Japanese Quince" or just "Japonica", from the old Latin name *Cydonia japonica*. Attractive flowers wreathe the stems both before leaf break and after they unfurl for weeks in early spring, followed, in the case of many cultivars, by fragrant ornamental fruits. These can be used for jellies although the true fruiting quince is better for edible purposes.

Seedlings of *Chaenomeles speciosa* are sometimes sold cheaply but are poor things in flower value compared to named cultivars. *C.s.* 'Nivalis' has large white flowers; *C.s.* 'Simonii' has blood-red flowers and spreading growth suited to banks. Excepting 'Simonii', the speciosa type and hybrids reach 3m height and 2–3m spread against walls.

More dense and rounded in habit, to 1.5m high and spread, are the *C. x superba* cultivars which can be grown both free-standing and against walls. *C. x s.* 'Crimson and Gold' AGM has stunning blood-red flowers and yellow anthers; *C. x s.* 'Lemon and Lime' opens ivory-white from March to May and has yellow fruits: *C. x s.* 'Nicoline' AGM has scarlet flowers on a plant of lower, more spreading habit; *C. x s.* 'Pink Lady' AGM is deep pink in bud opening rose pink; and *C. x s.* 'Rowallane' AGM is free-flowering with large crimson flowers. There are orange kinds too but nothing beats the reds on north walls. The strong thorns encourage their use in public

Tip

Well budded shoots can be cut late winter and forced indoors in water to provide early cut flowers.

Cercis siliquastrum

Chaenomeles superba 'Pink Lady'

Chaenomeles x s. 'Crimson and Gold'

Chaenomeles speciosa 'Nivalis'

places where vandals are a problem and they also form a good barrier to keep out animals.

The low growing cultivars are good ground cover plants for public gardens, street side planting and hot, sunny banks. Where exposed to hot sun on the more fertile soils they produce large quantities of flower. Occasionally it may be necessary to hack back old, overgrown plantings to clean them up and rejuvenate growth.

Cultivation

Chaenomeles are bullet-hardy, deciduous and thrive in all soils and sites, even the dry conditions close to walls.

Pruning is best undertaken during summer, after flowering. The next year's flowering spurs are encouraged by cutting back young new shoots to a few centimetres, rather like summer pruning apples. An ideal treatment for wall trained plants which may need this pruning as well as pruning back after flowering. In practice little pruning is necessary, especially if stems are cut for indoor decoration.

Propagation is by seed sown when ripe and kept in a cold frame. The seedlings will take up to five years to flower and many resulting plants are very poor. Named cultivars are propagated by cuttings 10cm long taken from side shoots, ideally with a heel of old bark, in July/August and by layering in September.

Netting may be needed to prevent birds pecking the buds. Plants infected with fire blight should be dug out and burnt.

Yellowing leaves are a symptom of insufficient iron and iron sequestrene watered on the soil in spring should control it.

CHIMONANTHUS

CHIMONANTHUS

Chimonanthus bears the perfect common name, "Winter Sweet", a deciduous shrub with willow-like leaves and fragrant flowers from December to February. *C. praecox* is hardy and has tubular-to-cup-shaped flowers 2cm across, yellow on the outside with purple-red throat. Found less commonly are *C.p.* 'Grandiflorus' AGM with deeper yellow petals with red centre and *C.p.* 'Luteus' AGM with large pale yellow flowers.

Cultivation

The twiggy, bushy growth of *Chimonanthus* reaches 3m in height and spread in well-drained soils, including chalk. A sunny position is best and against a south or west-facing wall it flowers earlier and for a longer period. Be patient, it can take several years for the wood to mature enough to flower.

Any pruning is best done in February, in practice cutting sprigs in flower to take indoors in winter is all they need.

New plants are propagated from ripe seed sown in October, for species and for named cultivars layer in September. The layers may take two years to root.

Choisya ternata 'Sundance'

CHOISYA

"Mexican Orange Blossom" is the common and very suitable name for *Choisya ternata*. In spring heavenly fragrance from the flowers makes it ideal for patios and beds beneath windows. The shiny dark green leaves are also aromatic when crushed.

Popular cultivars are *C.t.* 'Sundance' AGM with bright yellow ageing to deep golden leaves; and *C.* 'Aztec Pearl' AGM, a cross between *C. ternata* and *C. californica*. The last mentioned has narrower, paler green leaves and clusters of flowers pink in bud and white when fully open.

Tip

'Sundance' looks especially bright in winter against a hedge backdrop of light brown beech leaves.

Chimonanthus praecox

Choisya ternata

Cultivation

In mild and sheltered gardens *Choisya ternata* will grow to 2m in height and spread. While tolerant of some shade, it is best grown in full sun. In cold areas it requires the protection of a wall to reduce damage by wind and frost.

The green-leaved kinds, are best in full sun but tolerant of some shade. Any well-cultivated garden soil is suitable but it needs to be free-draining in winter. It is advisable to feed in spring, especially *C.t.* 'Sundance', to get brightly coloured foliage.

Pruning involves no more than the removal of frost-damaged shoots in spring. New shoots are freely produced from the base when plants are cut back. 'Sundance' can show some leaf browning and pruning off at this time removes flower bud.

Propagation is by half-ripe cuttings in July/August. These are best protected by glass over winter and planted out in spring.

Cultivation

All *Cistus* are ideal plants for hot sunny banks, borders and seaside planting. Drought is unlikely to harm them although waterlogging in heavy soils and severe frost in winter will cause losses.

Always plant pot-grown stock because they do not take kindly to root damage.

The only pruning is trimming back frost-damaged shoots.

Propagate as for *Choisya*.

CISTUS

There are over 30 species of evergreen *Cistus*, commonly called "Rock Rose" and "Sun Rose", usually growing no more than 1m high and the majority not being hardy. They produce masses of poppy-like single flowers, many of which have yellow or chocolate markings at the base. While each bloom is short-lived there are lots of them, from May to July.

Cistus x *aguilarii* 'Maculatus' AGM is a large white with crimson centre; *C.* x *corbariensis* AGM, crimson buds open white; *C.* x *purpureus* AGM purple pink and chocolate centre; *C.* x *pulverulentus* 'Sunset' deep pink; are freely available.

CLEMATIS:

see over, pages 56–57

CONVOLVULUS

A free-draining soil and sunny site is needed for the not completely hardy *Convolvulus cneorum* AGM. An attractive silver-leaved rock garden shrub, this has pink buds opening white from May to September.

Cultivation

Convolvulus cneorum will eventually reach 0.6m in height and spread.

No pruning is required and plants are propagated from half-ripe cuttings with a heel taken from June to August.

Cistus x *corbariensis*

Convolvulus cneorum

CLEMATIS

One of the most popular of all garden plants, *Clematis* species quite rightly deserve a book to themselves: another title in this series, 'Making the Most of Clematis' by Raymond Evison, the internationally renowned clematis specialist, fully meets that need. Here we do no more than introduce some of the more popular types and explain how they can be grown.

Early (April/May) and later (August/October) in the year we rely on the smaller-flowered kinds for garden colour. *Clematis alpina* has single pendula flowers consisting of four petals (on clematis these are correctly called tepals, being a combination of sepal – the green leaf-like pieces enclosing most flower buds – and petals). Excellent examples are *C.a.* 'Frances Rivis' AGM with pale blue flowers and *C.a.* 'Helsingborg' AGM, purple-blue.

Choose *C. macropetala* for semi-double flowers, good cultivars being *C.m.* 'Markham's Pink' AGM and *C.m.* 'White Swan' AGM. Both species will grow to 3m in good soil.

Both *Clematis orientalis* 'Bill Mackenzie' (syn. *C.* 'Bill Mackenzie') AGM and *C. tangutica* have bell-

Cultivation

All *clematis* grow well in reasonable garden soil, including chalky types. Where plenty of organic material, such as well-rotted manure or compost has been dug in to provide moisture in summer, they will grow and flower much better. Fed – rose fertilisers are ideal – and watered well in summer, they will abundantly repay the extra attention.

Prune spring-flowering types lightly after flowering, prune summer flowering kinds occasionally after flowering – hard pruning will delay flowering in the following year – prune late-summer-flowering cultivars hard back in early spring.

Propagation is by rooting softwood inter-nodal cuttings, i.e. the bottom cut being made between nodes, not as is usual just below a node, where leaf joins stem. Dip the cut end in rooting hormone chemical and root in frames with bottom heat in summer.

Wilt disease can be a problem on summer-flowering kinds. Watering the base of young plants with systemic fungicide in May will help control it.

shaped deep yellow single flowers from July to October, the former nearly double the flower size of the latter at up to 8cm across. They will grow 5–6m in height and spread. All of these are very hardy and the flowers followed by fluffy seed heads.

The most popular of all the smaller-flowered types, however, is *C. montana* and its cultivars, flowering in May/June. This is very vigorous, covering fences for 10m in length and growing up trees to a similar height in favourable sites and soils. Good cultivars are *C.m.* 'Elizabeth' AGM, scented soft pink; *C.m.* 'Grandiflora' AGM scented white flowers 8cm across; and *C.m.* 'Tetrarose' AGM, deep rosy-mauve.

There are very many large-flowered hybrids blooming from June to September, according to kind. Popular cultivars include: *C.* 'Duchess of Edinburgh', double white, scented, May/June and August/September, growing to 2.5m; *C.* 'Ernest Markham'

Clematis 'Nelly Moser'

Clematis alpina 'Frances Rivis'

Clematis viticella 'Etoile Violette'

AGM, deep red, June–September to 3.5m; C. 'Jackmanii' AGM, deep purple, July–September to 3m; C. 'Lasurstern' AGM, lavender-blue to 2.5m; C. 'Nelly Moser' AGM very pale mauve with deeper bar, May/June and August/September, to 2.5m, needing to be kept out of sun for best colour; and C. 'Niobe' AGM, dark blood-red, June–August, 2.5m, good in containers.

Smaller, more delicate flowers are provided in late summer by C. *viticella*, with single bell-shaped flowers, many having a white or paler star-shaped colouring to the inner petals. These grow well over heathers, up among early-sumer-flowering shrubs such as lilac and over lower-growing junipers. C.*v.* 'Minuet' AGM, white with mauve veining, July–August to 3m; and C.*v.* 'Etoile de Violette' AGM, violet-purple, July–September, 3–4m are well-tried cultivars.

Where the shelter of a south wall can be provided the less hardy C. *armandii*, creamy-white scented flowers, March–April, evergreen, to 6m; and C. *cirrhosa*, cream scented flowers December–February, evergreen, to 3m can be grown.

Clematis macropetala 'Markhams' Pink'

Clematis montana

CORNUS

CORNUS

Some *Cornus* have colourful barks but this is not the origin of their common name "Dogwood"! *Cornus* from the Latin indicates horny toughness which is the reason stems were used for dags, goads and skewers. Dag has over the years become dog.

The most widely used and easiest to grow are forms of *Cornus alba* and *Cornus stolonifera*. They vary in vigour, thrive in all soils and reach maximum size in moist conditions. Strongest and hardiest of all is *Cornus alba*, the "Siberian Dogwood", a suckering plant reaching 3m in height with red bark on young wood and mid-green leaves which colour in autumn before they fall.

Better garden forms include: *C.a.* 'Elegantissima' AGM with very attractive silver to white and green variegated leaves and red stems; *C.a.* 'Kesselringii' young leaves chestnut and stems dark purple to black; *C.a.* 'Sibirica' AGM, the "Westonbirt Dogwood" with brilliant crimson young bark in winter; *C.a.* 'Sibirica Variegata', similar to 'Elegantissima' although more compact with pink tinge to young leaves and the tendency to produce blue-green fruits tipped white on the ends of branches; *C.a.* 'Spaethii' AGM, red bark and golden variegated leaves all summer, best seen in the L.A.79 selections.

A good contrast to the red stems is *C. stolonifera* 'Flaviramea' AGM, the "Yellow-stemmed Dogwood" reaching 2m with green leaves in summer turning bright yellow before falling to expose the yellow to lime-green bark. *C. sanguinea* 'Winter Beauty' (syn. *C.s.* 'Winter Flame') gives the best of both worlds with orange and yellow bark on compact plants.

Tip

Plant *Cornus alba* 'Spaethii' where you want yellow foliage in full sun all summer. Unlike some yellow-leaved shrubs it does not scorch in full sun.

Cultivation

For those *Cornus* grown for colourful bark, chalky, wet, heavy and waterlogged soils and either sun or partial shade are suitable.

Once planted they are best left for at least two summers to become established. Thereafter pruning really hard back every other spring ensures masses of new growth and the brightest coloured bark.

Hardwood cuttings taken in October and November, root outside in sandy soils very easily.

Cornus alba 'Elegantissima'

Cornus alba 'Sibirica'

Now, four cornus species grown for flowers and foliage which make from tall shrubs to small trees. C. controversa has layered branches, alternate leaves and white flowers June/July, C.c. 'Variegata' AGM is less vigorous and even more attractive with white edges to the oval leaves.

The "Flowering Dogwood" of North America, *Cornus florida* is winter-hardy but needs autumn sun to ripen growth and no late spring frost. Their coloured bracts in May and autumn leaf colour are magnificent where the right growing conditions are provided, most likely in the east of England. C.f. 'Cherokee Chief' AGM has deep rose-red bracts and C.f. 'White Cloud' white bracts over bronzed foliage.

Cornus kousa is more suited to the British climate and eventually produces layers of four-bract white inflorescences in May/June. C.k. var. *chinensis* AGM has smooth edged larger leaves and bracts and good autumn leaf colour on some soils. It needs a well drained and sunny site.

Cornus mas AGM, the "Cornelian Cherry" is grown for the mass of small yellow flowers on bare branches in February and March. C.m. 'Aurea' has yellow leaves in early summer and C.m. 'Variegata' AGM has creamy-white variegated leaves. Both cultivars are more free-fruiting than the species and the yellow and crimson cherry-like fruits can be used in preserves.

Cultivation
None of the four *Cornus* grown for their flowers requires pruning, all are generally trouble-free.

C. mas can be seed raised, the remainder are propagated by half-ripe cuttings – ideally with a heel – under mist in July and August.

Cornus mas

Cornus controversa 'Variegata'

COROKIA

COROKIA

Somewhat tender shrubs from New Zealand, *Corokia cotoneaster* has small and spare evergreen leaves and angular, sparse intertwined branches to 2.5m which prompt the common name "Wire-netting Bush". Yellow flowers in spring are followed by orange fruits. *C. x virgata* is a bit hardier and reaches 4m.

Cultivation
Corokia will spread in sheltered gardens and in poor soil as long as it is well drained. Little pruning is needed and they are propagated by layering or half-ripe cuttings under glass in summer.

CORYLOPSIS

A light, pretty but not spectacular group of early-flowering shrubs, the pale yellow coswlip-scented blooms of which, hang like hazel catkins on the bare branches in March and April. *Corylopsis pauciflora* AGM reaches 1.5–2m in height and the flowers come in twos and threes.

Corokia

Cultivation
Corylopsis are good plants to grow on the edge of woodland and in shade. They need acid soil, little pruning and are propagated either by layering in the autumn or by half-ripe cuttings taken with a heel and rooted under glass.

CORYLUS

The first signs of spring are yellow male "Hazel" catkins on Britain's native nut *Corylus avellana*. Female flowers made up of red stigma tufts are hardly noticed and produce the nuts in October.

There are several close cousins which make useful garden shrubs including: *Corylus avellana* 'Contorta' with curiously twisted branches hence the common names "Corkscrew Hazel" and "Harry Lauder's Walking Stick"; *C.a.* 'Aurea', the "Golden Nut", with soft yellow leaves; *C. maxima* 'Purpurea', the "Purple Hazlenut" having large dark purple, almost black leaves and purple catkins 7.5–10cm long. *C. maxima* is the filbert with a longer nut and husk which completely covers it.

All can be planted in mixed borders, the purple and yellow contrasting if planted together, and the "Corkscrew Hazel" is best with a light background to throw up the twisted stems in winter.

Tip
A clump of hazel regularly coppiced will provide an excellent supply of poles to support runner beans and brush to support sweet peas and tall herbaceous plants.

Cultivation
Corylus grow in most soils, including chalk, and thrive in full sun and partial shade. Fruiting will be heavier on moderate rather than rich soil.

Prune if necessary after flowering in March when branches four or more years old can be cut out to stimulate new replacements. New plants are obtained from layers in autumn and by grafting *C.a.* 'Contorta'.

Corylopsis pauciflora

Corylus maxima 'Purpurea'

Corylus avellana 'Contorta'

Cultivation

Cotinus are easy to grow once established, they prefer full sun and a well-drained soil. Heavily manured rich soils are less likely to give good autumn colour. The best leaf colour is produced on current year's wood, so some pruning on established vigorous plants in March may be necessary. Propagate by layering low branches in September. Where soil conditions are dry mildew disease may be a problem, a systemic fungicide gives control.

COTINUS

Lovely deciduous shrubs, previously called *Rhus cotinus* and now *Cotinus coggygria* AGM (most easily pronounced as two strong syllables with emphasis on the y thus *cogg y gria*) and happily more frequently referred to as the "Smoke Tree" on account of the wispy flowers in June/July which turn smoke-grey and "Venetian Sumach".

Both species and cultivars have good autumn leaf colour and the bright yellow wood is used to provide dye. *Cotinus coggygria* AGM is a rounded shrub, eventually reaching 3m, the leaves green and the flowers light brown. *C.c.* 'Royal Purple' AGM has light purple leaves changing to red in the autumn,. *C.c.* 'Notcutt's Variety' is similar, both making a medium-sized shrub.

Much larger is *C. obovatus* AGM reaching 10m in its native South East USA, one of the parents of *C.* 'Grace' AGM which has large soft purple leaves that turn scarlet in autumn beneath purplish-pink summer flowers.

Tip
Underplanting purple-leaved *Cotinus* with a large-flowered clematis of appropriate colouring can be a very eye-catching display.

Cotinus coggygria

COTONEASTER

The Cotoneasters are amongst the most important hardy shrubs for both garden and landscape use. They come in many forms, from small trees through all sizes of shrubs down to ground-hugging ground coverers and rockery plants. Brilliant berries, mostly red but also yellow, and autumn foliage are their great strengths.

All carry an abundance of small pink-in-bud opening to white flowers in early summer. While they are listed under three headings here, it should be remembered that young vigorously-growing semi-evergreens will hold their leaves longer than older ones and hard winter weather causes earlier leaf fall.

EVERGREENS

The fully evergreen *Cotoneaster conspicuus* forms a dense mound of arching branches 2m in height and spread, the small bluish-green leaves hidden by the mass of red fruits in autumn. Lower growing and wider spreading is C.c. 'Decorus' AGM, a very free-fruiting form ideal for banks and rock garden use.

Even better for ground cover and bank carpeting is *C. dammeri* AGM which grows only a few centimetres high but each plant spreading to eventually cover four square metres. This can be planted in full sun or in shade beneath trees and taller shrubs, a good replacement for turf that will never need mowing. C.d. 'Coral Beauty' (syn. C. x *suecicus* 'Coral Beauty') is a free-fruiting similar form, with many bright red berries. It is also grafted on a short trunk to make an attractive small weeping tree.

One of the more common and taller weeping trees is C. *salicifolius* 'Pendulus'. This takes a little time to train up on a 1.2–2m trunk but once

Cotoneaster frigidus

established creates an eye-catching feature when the branches are strung with red berries.

One of the best evergreen hedge plants is C. *lacteus* AGM, flowering freely in June/July and ripening later than most to provide many large clusters or red berries well into the winter. It will reach 3m high and with regular trimming can be kept quite narrow.

A real toughie is C. *microphyllus* AGM with tiny evergreen leaves which are an excellent foil to the large globular crimson fruits. Grow this against walls and use it to cover fences and uneven ground where a tidy, attractive look with the minimum of maintenance is required.

Largest in this group is C. *salicifolius* which reaches 4–5m in height and spread. The graceful arching branches are formed in layers and covered in bright berries each autumn. It has produced several

Cotoneaster dammeri

Cotoneaster microphyllus

cultivars such as C.*s.* 'Autumn Fire' (syn. C.*s.* 'Herbstfeuer') with weeping habit, willow-like leaves and masses of bright red berries – suitable for ground cover and trained up to form a weeping tree – and C.*s.* 'Rothschildianus' AGM with large creamy yellow fruits on a large spreading shrub.

SEMI-EVERGREEN

As the group heading indicates the demarcation between these groups is somewhat blurred.

Cotoneaster bullatus AGM has less dense upright growth to 2m carrying large, deeply wrinkled dark green leaves. These turn scarlet in the autumn when branches carry crimson fruits. C. 'Cornubia' (syn. C. *frigidus* 'Cornubia') grows to 6m or more, vigorous enough to be offered on a trunk to form a full standard tree. The

COTONEASTER

original plant at Exbury exceeded 8m x 6m and produced some of the largest fruits of the genus, literally weighing down the branches.

On a smaller scale and even more elegant is *C. sternianus* AGM, sage green leaves having a silver underside which gives a crisp outline to each leaf, an excellent foil to the bright orange fruits. This species makes an excellent tub plant for patio decoration and is able to withstand some drought.

While a number of cotoneasters are used for hedging, *C. simonsii* AGM is best known for this purpose. Very upright growth to 2m and more, the green leaves turning red in autumn before they fall to expose scarlet berries held close to the stem.

Cotoneaster x *watereri* is a group of cultivars of mixed parentage, the result of crosses between *C. frigidus*, *C. henryanus* and *C. salicifolius*. One of the best examples is *C. x w.* 'John Waterer' AGM.

DECIDUOUS

Perhaps best known of all is *Cotoneaster horizontalis* AGM, the "Fishbone Cotoneaster" common name describing well the shape of the branches. An invaluable plant to cover all walls, even those facing north and east, to 2m in height and up to 4m spread. It is excellent on banks and has rich autumn leaf colour as well as lots of scarlet berries.

C.h. 'Variegatus' AGM (syn *C. atropurpureus* 'Variegatus') has leaves edged white and is less vigorous; *Cotoneaster adpressus* AGM is a dwarf wide-spreading shrub; and finally *C. divaricatus* makes a medium-sized shrub with good autumn colour and lots of dark red fruits, another good hedge plant.

Cotoneaster horizontalis

Cotoneaster lacteus

Cultivation

Cotoneaster these shrubs are very easy to grow and thrive in all garden soils, preferably not waterlogged in winter. They do remarkably well in quite dry soils and both deciduous and the lower growing evergreens fruit better in full sun. Space *C. simonsii* 30–50cm apart and *C. lacteus* to 1–2m apart for hedging.

Most are left unpruned to develop their natural shape. If they get too large cut full branches away, the evergreens in April, the deciduous in February. Evergreen kinds grown as hedges need vigorous shoots and side growths pruned back after flowering. Ideally, prune back to the nearest cluster of berries. Most of them respond well to really hard pruning occasionally to rejuvenate the bush.

Species can be propagated from seed sown as soon as it is ripe, but beware, cross pollination is likely to give variation. Take heel cuttings of evergreens in late August and September, half-ripe cuttings of deciduous kinds in July/August. If you have difficulty layer low branches in October and November. Fireblight causes a blackening of the foliage, progressing back from the branch tip. Infected plants are best dug out and burn to prevent spread of this disease.

CRATAEGUS

The thorn, *Crataegus monogyna* is well known by the common names "May", its flowering time, and "Quickthorn". The flowers are followed by scarlet berries. It is a mixture of *C. monogyna* crossed with *C. laevigata* (syn. *C. oxyacantha*) which produces the popular double flowering thorn trees such as *C.l.* 'Paul's Scarlet' AGM.

Common seedling quickthorns make an excellent hedge, both trimmed repeatedly to provide a low garden hedge and allowed free rein to make an impenetrable farm field hedge. For even fiercer thorns and larger fruits *C. coccinea*, the "Scarlet Haw" should be chosen.

The "Glastonberry Thorn", *C. mollis* 'Biflora' a large shrub to small tree which sprouts into growth much earlier than other species and occasionally produces a light crop of small flowers in winter. Its main flowering is late spring followed by dark red berries.

All are very hardy, once established withstanding drought, exposure and some waterlogging.

Cultivation

Most soils are suitable and while they tolerate shade, flowering and fruiting is better in sunlight. Always keep the roots damp when transplanting, if allowed to dry they are slow to break into growth.

Space hedge plants 30–45cm apart, pruning back bare-root transplanted seedlings to encourage base branching. When overgrown they respond well to pruning hard back, otherwise trim after flowering or in the autumn.

Hedge plants are raised from seed. Remove them from the flesh as soon as they are ripe. Sow either in the soil or in containers left exposed to frost and winter weather. Germination can take 18 months and longer. Named cultivars are grafted onto seedling rootstocks.

Crataegus monogyna

CYTISUS

CYTISUS

Tumbling sprays of flower like water from a fountain are provided by the "Brooms", both British native *Cytisus scoparius* and the many other species and hybrids which make excellent garden plants. All have small pea-shaped flowers and many are leafless for the greater part of the year. The arching green stems on many are a feature in themselves and coveted by flower arrangers who want a strong curving line in their designs.

Closely related to *Genista* and *Spartium*, *Cytisus* is a genera of shrubs ranging from flat, spreading types to strong growers reaching four metres. Their common name, "Broom", comes from the use of branches for sweeping. While the green stems are quite dramatic, the leaves are small, either in three parts or single and for the most part are only on the stems for a short period each year, if at all.

Best known in gardens are the May-flowering hybrids from several species and coloured forms of *Cytisus scoparius* such as *C.s. andreanus* AGM, yellow and crimson; C. 'Golden Sunlight', rich yellow; C. 'Goldfinch', gold and claret; all growing 2m or more in height and spread. Among the species hybrids are some excellent garden plants including C. 'Hollandia' AGM, cream and pink flowers; C. 'Lena' AGM raised at Kew, deep red, red and yellow, more compact at 1.3m; and C. 'Zeelandia' AGM, lilac and cream with wings of flowers pinkish cream.

More suited to rockeries is C. x *beanii* AGM, 30cm in height and 0.8–1m spread with golden yellow flowers in May. Even lower-growing and wider-spreading is C. x *kewensis* AGM, an excellent ground cover plant with creamy white flowers.

My favourite brooms are C. x *praecox*, the "Warminster Broom" and its form C. x *p.* 'Albus' and C. x *p.* 'Allgold' AGM. These flower April/May and produce a neat rounded habit, their scent being heavy, not really pleasant so best planted a little way from the house.

C. *purgans* is chalk-tolerant, has dense, erect almost rush-like growth to 1.3m and fragrant yellow flowers in May. C. x *purpureus* (also called *Chamaecytisus*) grows little more than 1.5m in height and spread, with purple flowers in May/June. C.p. *albus* is a white form and C.p. 'Atropur-pureus' AGM has deep purple flowers.

Cytisus battandierii AGM is an exception, growing to 5m in height and spread to small tree size. It has large silver-green laburnum-like leaves and upright clusters of rich yellow pineapple-scented flowers. A fine shrub, this "Moroccan Broom" needs the protection of a west wall in colder northern British gardens.

Cytisus x *praecox* 'Allgold'

Cytisus 'Hollandia'

Cultivation

With the exception of *Cytisus battandieri* which needs some protection in the north, all the above are easy to grow, free-flowering and very hardy. They are happy in a wide range of soils including chalk, but are best in well-drained, poor rather than rich soil and in full sun.

Most of them grow well with no pruning, the hybrids are more shapely if the immediate past season's growth is sheared back by half immediately after flowering. Old plants which have become woody do not take kindly to hard pruning.

Species are raised from seed sown in April in a cold frame. Named cultivars are propagated by side stems pulled off with a heel of older growth in August/September and rooted in sandy soil in a cold frame.

A gall mite causes strange growth on the stems, where this occurs, especially in the south of England, cut them off and burn.

Cytisus battandieri

Cytisus kewensis

DANAE

The "Alexandrian Laurel", *Danae racemosa*, AGM differs from its close relative "Butcher's Broom" (*Ruscus*) in being thornless and bisexual so that every plant may carry berries in the autumn and winter. It grows to about 0.6m high and spreads bamboo-like, the stiff stems carrying small polished green leaves. The small yellowy-green flowers are insignificant but in hot summers are followed by orange-red fruits.

Danae racemosa

Daphne mezereum

Cultivation

An excellent low shrub for moist soils and shady places, it also provides useful evergreen foliage that remains attractive for a long time when cut and kept in water.

Propagation is by seed and division in spring.

DAPHNE

Delightfully fragrant flowering plants, both evergreen and deciduous, *Daphne* are cherished garden plants. Some can be frustrating, however, growing well in some sites and soils while proving difficult to establish a stone's throw away.

Daphne bholua is semi-evergreen and can reach 3m but needs shelter, such as that provided by a south facing wall. It produces pale purple-pink flowers, scented somewhat of lemons, in small clusters from late December to March, followed by black fruits.

The clone *D.b.* 'Gurkha' AGM with pale mauve-to-white flowers is very fragrant, evergreen and much hardier.

Cultivar *D.b.* 'Jacqueline Postill' AGM is evergreen and has larger flowers over a longer period, growing to 4m. Chalky soils may turn the leaves chlorotic, more acidic conditions and some acid fertiliser will be needed to green them up.

Not the most spectacular in flower, *Daphne* x *burkwoodii* AGM has very fragrant soft pink flowers in rounded groups on leafy spurs for weeks in May/June. It grows to 1m in height and spread and is most commonly found as the clone *D.* x *b.* 'Somerset', which is a little more vigorous.

Most common of all is *D. mezereum*, valuable for its deliciously scented flowers on bare upright stems in February and March. Even in the most favourable sites, maximum height is unlikely to exceed 1m. Flowers are followed by spectacular

Most Daphnes are native to limestone and alkaline conditions but they do well in rich, well-drained soils which are not too acid. The ideal site is a good, free-draining sandy loam, moist in summer, and in full sun. I have, however, seen them growing well in heavy clay soils so this is one plant worth the gamble whatever the soil type.

All transplant poorly and are best established from young pot-grown plants. Old gardeners used to say, "Daphnes shrink from the knife" and they are better not pruned. Any straggly shoots which have to be removed should be cut off in March. Don't be afraid to pinch out the growing tips of young D. odora types to produce well-branched plants.

Propagation is by seed, cuttings and layers. Raise seedlings from Daphne mezereum by picking the seed as it ripens, removing the flesh and sowing immediately. Cuttings of D. odora are made from sideshoots of the current year's growth, ideally with a heel, from July to September and rooting in cold frames. Virus diseases can be a problem so spray to kill greenfly, which spread such viruses.

poisonous scarlet berries. There are rose pink and white forms, the latter producing amber berries. Where these plants flower and fruit very heavily they can be short-lived.

One of the easiest and best Daphne for small gardens is D. odora, an evergreen eventually reaching 1.5m in height and up to 2m spread. This needs a sheltered spot and for colder gardens D.o. 'Aureomarginata' should be chosen. This form withstands temperatures down to 22°F (−5°C), the leaves are attractively edged creamy white and the purple-red buds open to almost white in February and March and are very fragrant.

DEUTZIA

Deutzia is one of those easy growing shrubs which, given space, can be quite stunning in full flower. Two good hybrid cultivars, growing 1.8m high and spreading to 1.5m, are D. 'Magicien' with large pink-tinted flowers with white edge and purple band on the back and D. 'Mont Rose" AGM, a free-flowering rose and deep rose pink,

Smaller in size to 1.2m is D. x elegantissima 'Rosealind' AGM with deep carmine flowers on arching stems. Smaller in size to 1m or less is D. x rosea which has the delicate characteristics of its more tender parent D. gracilis, a good species to

Deutzia 'Mont Rose'

flower early in pots in a conservatory. D. x rosea 'Carminea' AGM grows a little larger and has white flowers with purple outer edges to the petals. D. scabra grows erect to 3.5m tall with the bark peeling from older branches. D.s. 'Plena' has double flowers tinted rose purple and D. magnifica is a good double white.

Cultivation

All good soils are suitable for Deutzia including some lime, an open sunny site will give the best-shaped growth but some shade from hot sun helps the pink flowers to hold their colour. Prune some old stems out after flowering.

Propagation is either from half-ripe cuttings in July/August or hardwood cuttings in October.

Daphne odora 'Aureomarginata'

Deutzia magnifica

ELAEAGNUS

Elaeagnus x ebbingei 'Gilt Edge'

ELAEAGNUS

While there are more than 30 species of deciduous and evergreen *Elaeagnus*, two, *E. x ebbingei* and *E. pungens* make superb garden subjects and are excellent evergreens for tubs.

Working through the more popular shrubs alphabetically, *E. angustifolia* AGM makes a large shrub or small tree to 12m with deciduous willow-like leaves dull green above, silver beneath. It has fragrant flowers in June followed by 13mm long oval fruits silvery-amber in colour.

A more useful and very hardy garden plant is *E. commutata*, the "Thornless Silver Berry", with upright slender branches to 3m and bright silver leaves. Small silvery flowers in May are fragrant and followed by small silver berries.

Among the most popular are cultivars of *E. x ebbingei*, a species cross between *E. macrophylla*, a robust

Cultivation

Elaeagnus are not demanding and grow well in most soils. Avoid shallow chalky soils and plant in fertile conditions for the best-coloured foliage.

Where you need to reshape prune in June and if necessary again in the autumn. Usually the only pruning needed occurs when foliage is cut for flower arrangement. Be sure to prune out shoots on variegated kinds which revert to green.

Evergreens are propagated from half-ripe cuttings made from young side shoots rooted under mist nozzles in summer. Deciduous kinds are raised from seed sown in frames when ripe in July/August.

evergreen, *E. pungens* and *E. x reflexa.* It is quite fast-growing, has large evergreen leaves mid-green above, silver beneath and small off-white fragrant flowers in November on mature wood. Their perfume really fills the air and, hidden from view under the leaves, many people wonder where it is coming from.

Variegated leaf forms provide year round colour especially with *E. x e.* 'Gilt Edge' AGM which has deep green leaves edged gold, growing to 2m and *E. x e.* 'Limelight', its large green leaves having a central blotch of yellow, to 3m.

Not quite as hardy are the *E. pungens* cultivars, *E.p.* 'Maculata' AGM, dark green with central splash of yellow, and less commonly offered *E.p.* 'Dicksonii' green with golden yellow margin and *E.p.* 'Frederici' the smaller of the three with cream-edged-bright-green leaves.

All are excellent for mixed shrub borders, to grow as single specimens and lightly trimmed to make an informal hedge. *E. x ebbingei* makes a good wind-protecting screen even in coastal areas.

Elaeagnus x ebbingei

Elaeagnus pungens 'Maculata'

ENKIANTHUS

This erectly-branched deciduous shrub can reach 4m and requires an acid soil. *Enkianthus campanulatus* AGM is grown for its classy pale yellowish-bronze clusters of bell-shaped flowers and especially for the yellow and scarlet autumn leaf colour.

Cultivation
Enkianthus grow well in both sun and partial shade.

They need little pruning and are propagated from 7cm cuttings taken August/September and rooted in a frame.

ERICA – see heathers

ESCALLONIA

The almost evergreen foliage of *Escallonia* is good foil to the clusters of flowers produced throughout the summer and early autumn ranging from white, pale pink to crimson. In very hardy winter weather many will drop their leaves and in extremely frosty conditions stems can be killed by frost.

Among many excellent garden hybrids are a number raised in Northern Ireland which carry the raiser Slieve Donard's name. Many come from crosses between *E. virgata* and *E. rubra* or its variety *E.r. macrantha*, one long-established example being *E.* 'Langleyensis' AGM, growing to 2.5m, rose-pink. It is a parent of *E.* 'Apple Blossom' AGM slower-growing to 1.8m which in turn produced the deeper pink *E.* 'Peach Blossom' AGM and the red early-flowering *E.* 'Pride of Donard' AGM which has glossier dark green leaves.

An improvement on *E.r. macrantha* is *E.* 'Donard Radiance' AGM which has large rich pink flowers on erect branches to 1.8m a

Enkianthus campanulatus

good seaside plant. *E.* 'Donard Seedling' has arching branches to 3m, large leaves and pink buds opening white. *E.* 'Edinensis' AGM is hardier than *E.* 'Langleyensis' with arching branches to 2m and deep pink buds opening to shell pink. Later-flowering is *E.* 'Iveyi' AGM to 3m whose glossy leaves are somewhat aromatic when crushed and is not so hardy away from the coast.

A good garden cultivar is *E.* 'Red Elf' with compact habit and crimson flowers in June, an offspring from the

Cultivation
Escallonia grows well in moist garden conditions including alkaline and also survive drought in light, free-draining soils. Those planted in cold northern gardens away from the coast benefit from fence and wall protection. In warm moist conditions they often flower a second time in the autumn.

Any pruning to thin out congested branches is best undertaken after early summer flowering.

more vigorous *E.* 'C.F. Ball', rich red to 2–3m. *E.r.* 'Crimson Spire' AGM and *E.* 'Red Hedger' have excellent wind and salt spray resistance so are good for coastal screening. Escallonias make good less formal hedges when spaced 0.5m apart.

Tip
Be patient with established plants that appear to have been killed by frost, given time they usually grow again from the base.

Escallonia 'Peach Blossom'

EUCALYPTUS

There are hundreds of *Eucalyptus* species growing as tall trees. Several respond well to annual early spring pruning to form medium-sized shrubs. They provide very useful foliage to cut and use fresh in flower arrangements or treat with glycerine for dried flower arrangements.

Eucalyptus gunii AGM, the "Cedar Gum", is fast-growing, the juvenile leaves rounded and silver-blue, then as the plant ages the foliage changes to the adult green sickle-shaped leaves.

Cultivation

Annual pruning after the chance of hard frost retains the more attractive juvenile leaves.

Eucalyptus reaches 2m in a season as established stooled shrubs.

Propagation is from seed which for Britain needs to be of a hardy strain.

Eucalyptus gunii

EUCRYPHIA

While considered tender, once well established *Eucryphia glutinosa* AGM proves a fairly hardy deciduous or partially evergreen shrub.

It will eventually reach 3m and over but is slow-growing and has rich glossy green leaves as a foil to show off the single white flowers and massed yellow-tipped stamens in July/August.

E. x *nymansensis* 'Nymansay" AGM eventually makes a small upright evergreen tree with 6cm flowers in late summer-early autumn.

Cultivation

Eucryphia need a soil with plenty of organic matter and a sheltered site in sun or partial shade.

Propagate from half-ripe cuttings in August/September under glass or raise from seed or layers.

Eucryphia glutinosa

EUONYMUS

A useful group of deciduous and evergreen shrubs with *Euonymus alatus* AGM having an open, stiff habit with narrow oval green leaves on four-winged, corky-barked stems. It grows to 2m with branches spreading out horizontally.

Insignificant greenish May/June flowers are followed by purple fruits, red seeds and excellent autumn colour before the leaves fall in autumn. *E.a.* 'Compactus' AGM is a shorter, denser form useful for low hedges.

The wild "Spindle Tree", *Euonymus europaeus,* was used for spindles in weaving and is well known for its green wood, brilliant autumn leaf colour and, where cross-pollination occurs, rose-red four-lobed seed capsules enclosing orange seeds. Even brighter is the garden form selected by the late Rowland Jackman called *E.e.* 'Red Cascade' AGM with 2m high stems thickly clustered with fruits that

Euonymus europaeus 'Red Cascade'

Euonymus japonicus 'Ovatus Aureus'

Euonymus fortunei radicans 'Silver Queen'

grow and then climbing to a metre or two when they reach a vertical support. Like the ivies, flowers form on mature stems.

Among a score or more cultivars, are: *E.f.r.* 'Emerald Gaiety' AGM, deep green with white edges to the leaves that turn pinkish in winter; *E.f.r.* 'Emerald n' Gold' AGM, bright yellow and green tinged bronzey-pink in winter; *E.f.r.* 'Silver Queen' AGM, compact-growing plant, green edged creamy white, again tinted pink in cold weather; and *E.f.r.* 'Sunspot', slightly taller, to 0.5m, with larger leaves dark green with deep yellow splash. They can be trimmed to form low box-like hedges.

Much taller and free-standing are *Euonymus japonicus* cultivars which are not entirely hardy but grow well in pots, in protected gardens and in coastal areas. They are grown for their bold attractive leaves which thrive in city grime. *E.j.* 'Latifolius Albo-marginatus' AGM has mid-green leaves with bold white margins and *E.j.* 'Ovatus Aureus' AGM is the most commonly seen, with lighter green cream and yellow leaves, the brightest coloured in full sun.

set well even on isolated plants.

Much more popular are the evergreens, especially cultivars of *E. fortunei radicans* growing in some ways similar to ivies, the stems spreading across the ground, rooting as they

EXORCHORDA

Hardy and deciduous *Exochorda* x *macrantha* 'The Bride' AGM is a graceful shrub flowering freely in April/May.

Exochorda x macrantha 'The Bride'

Cultivation

Euonymus grow well in all soils, even poor dry ones over chalk.

E.f. radicans cultivars are excellent ground cover plants in sun and shade, even surviving strong competition from tree roots Both evergreens grow well in containers, the *radicans* especially useful in window boxes and hanging baskets in winter.

Deciduous types need little more than the occasional thinning of old branches in February. The evergreens can be trimmed in April and August/September. When ground cover plants look straggly just shear hard back in spring and feed them well to rejuvenate them.

Raise from seed and all can be rooted from cuttings taken with a heel of mature wood in August/September in frames. All the evergreens root easily from tip cuttings in July/August.

Mildew disease can infect the leaves in dry conditions but a fungicidal spray soon cures it. Black fly overwinter on the spindle tree and should be sprayed in spring to prevent it spreading to broad beans.

Cultivation

Exochorda grows in most soils except shallow chalk and can be rooted from soft cuttings in heat under glass. Any pruning is done after flowering.

FALLOPIA

FALLOPIA

Previously called *Polygonum*, *Fallopia baldschuanica* AGM is better known by the common name "Russian Vine" or more appropriately "Mile-a-Minute". One of the most rampant deciduous climbers, it is ideal to do a massive screening job.

Once established, five metres' extension a year is commonplace.

Cultivation

Almost any site and soil is suitable, including chalk.

Pruning is hardly the word, jungle warfare hacking back in winter is a better description.

Fallopia baldshuanica is rooted from soft wood cuttings.

Fallopia baldschuanica

FATSIA

A popular house plant, *Fatsia japonica* AGM, the "False Caster-Oil Plant" is also a hardy shrub, ideal for shady spots and to grow in containers. It is grown for its large leathery palm-shaped shiny green leaves. Star Wars-like flowers explode into globes of spiky ivory-coloured heads of bloom from October, followed by black berries.

There is a variegated form *F.j.* 'Variegata' AGM with white edges to the leaves. It can be used in mixed borders, as a specimen for dramatic architectural effect and in patio pots.

Cultivation

Here's a plant for all soils, one which survives city dirt and is best sheltered from drying cold winter winds. Plants are raised from seed, from suckers carefully dug away from parent plants and by cuttings. No pruning is required but too-large plants respond well to hard pruning in April.

Fatsia japonica

Forsythia x intermedia 'Lynwood LA69'

FORSYTHIA

As much a part of spring in Britain as trumpet daffodils, the cultivars of *Forsythia* x *intermedia* growing to 2–3m are to be seen in every suburb. A cross between *F. suspensa* and *F. viridissima*, it has produced such good-natured garden plants as *F.* x *i.* 'Spectabilis' with branches packed with flower and a sport from it, *F.* x *i.* 'Lynwood LA69' AGM which has more upright growth.

Where space is limited seek out the more compact *F.* x *i.* 'Spring Glory' growing to 1.8m and *F.* x *i.* 'Minigold'. Much more lax in habit is *F. suspensa* AGM the stems of which, if cut through lengthways, will be found to have no pith between the leaf nodes. This grows 3–5m high and spreads to 3m and more, given the support of a wall or fence. For the best effect let it grow up one wall side and flow over the top and down the other side.

F. 'Week-End' flowers on old and the previous year's wood and cultivars with variegated foliage include *F.* 'Fiesta' from New Zealand and *F.* 'Sunflash'. *F. ovata* is earlier-flowering, from February, and compact-growing, to 1.5m, *F.o.* 'Tetragold' has large amber-yellow flowers.

Cultivation

All garden soils are suitable, forsythias thriving in exposed sites and city grime.

They flower best on young 2–3 year old branches so pruning out some old stems immediately after flowering is advisable.

Propagation is by hardwood cuttings in autumn. Sparrows can get a taste for the flower buds, where this happens netting the plant for a year should train them out of the habit.

Tip

Cut well-budded stems of *Forsythia* from late January onwards to force into flower early to provide useful long-lasting cut flowers. *Forsythia* x *intermedia* 'Golden Bells' is good for this flowering on one year wood.

Forsythia suspensa

Fremontodendron 'California Glory'

FOTHERGILLA

Related to "Witch Hazel", *Fothergilla major* AGM grows 2–3m high, has bottle-brush-like creamy flowers in April/May and glossy dark green leaves that colour brilliantly in autumn before they fall.

Fothergilla major

Cultivation

Fothergilla needs light, moist lime-free soil and is propagated by layers.

FREMONTODENDRON

A very long-lasting wall shrub, *Fremontodendron* 'California Glory' AGM needs the protection and support of a south- or west-facing wall.

Cultivation

Full sun, good draining and a not too fertile soil are needed for the best flowering.

Pruning is unnecessary save to retain size – wear gloves and eye protection when pruning to avoid irritation.

FUCHSIA

Fuchsia 'Mrs Popple'

FUCHSIA

Hardy fuchsias survive most winters in Britain and although branches can be killed by severe frost they usually shoot again from below ground in spring, to 1m in height. Where they are not frosted, in sheltered and warm coastal areas, branches reach 2–4m.

The most common and hardiest species is *Fuchsia magellanica* with long slender flowers, the calyx of four sepals scarlet and the skirt-like corolla or petals violet. *F.m.* var. *gracilis* AGM has very narrow leaves and slender scarlet and violet blooms. *F.m.* var. *pumila* is a tiny plant 15cm high with 1–2cm long red and purple flowers. *F.m.* 'Versicolor' AGM has grey-green leaves tinged pink when young and edged creamy white when fully developed. *F.* 'Riccartonii' AGM (syn. *F.m.* 'Riccartonii') is probably the most popular of all and was introduced in Edinburgh in 1854. Established plants will drip with slender scarlet and violet flowers from June to November.

Other well-tried hardy types with larger leaves include: *F.* 'Mrs Popple' AGM, large crimson and purple; *F.* 'Genii' AGM, red and violet blue; *F.* 'Madame Cornelissen" AGM, red and white; *F.* 'Margaret' AGM, crimson and purple, to 1.5m; and two good compact forms *F.* 'Lady Thumb' AGM to 0.4m, pink; and *F.* 'Tom Thumb', AGM 0.35m red and light purple flowers.

Fuchsia magellanica var. gracilis

Cultivation

All soils are suitable for Fuchsias but they need moisture in summer and free drainage in winter. The golden-leaved forms can scorch in hot sun and most grow well in partial shade.

Pruning should be left until spring, the mass of branches giving some frost protection. Once growth starts cut out all dead wood. To restrain height prune to a few inches each spring.

Propagation is by softwood cuttings, ideally of non-flowering shoots, April to June. Plant as early in summer as possible because well established specimens are better able to withstand frost. A mulch of dry peat or leaves around the crown in December will give a lot of protection from severe frost.

Fuchsia 'Lady Thumb'

GARRYA

The glossy ever-grey-green foliage of *Garrya elliptica* is as attractive as bay, equally able to withstand city grime and has the added benefit of long slender silver-green catkins in January/February. These turn yellow as pollen is released.

Choose G.*e*. 'James Roof' AGM, a male with catkins up to 18cm long. The female form is rarely seen and has purple-brown fruits.

Griselinia littoralis

Garrya elliptica

Cultivation

Cold winds can burn the leaves of *Garrya* in winter so ideally plant against walls, even north-facing ones, for some protection.

They grow well in all ordinary free-draining soils to 3m and can reach 5m. Always plant pot-grown specimens because root disturbance checks growth. Young plants will need protection in cold districts over winter until well established.

Pruning is likely to be executed when cutting branches for indoor decoration. Any other pruning back should be done in early spring.

Propagation is from half-ripe cuttings with bottom heat in late summer.

GENISTA

Closely related to *Cytisus* and having the same common name, "Broom", *Genista* provides a number of low-growing floriferous garden plants. *Genista aetnensis* AGM is the exception, growing to 5m with loose, open habit, rush-like foliage and yellow flowers July/August. This is the least hardy, unlike *Genista hispanica*, "Spanish Gorse", a tough semi-globular plant up to 1m in radius, densely spined and covered in yellow flowers in June.

Genista lydia AGM is much more broom-like, semi-prostrate reaching 1m spreading to 2m and festooned in yellow flowers in May/June. *Genista pilosa* 'Vancouver Gold' forms a dense low grey-green carpet to 0.3m high and spreading 1m or more.

Cultivation

Genista are easy to grow in full sun and any light, well-drained soil. They require little feeding and do not transplant well so always plant pot-raised plants.

They require no pruning save perhaps a little shaping after flowering and are propagated by half-ripe cuttings with a heel taken in August. Root these in sandy soil in a cold frame.

GRISELINIA

A somewhat tender evergreen from New Zealand, *Griselinia littoralis* AGM proves an excellent hedge and screening plant, especially for coastal gardens. G.*l*. 'Dixon's Cream' is a good variegated form.

Cultivation

Space *Griselinia* hedge plants 0.5m apart and shape them in April and/or August. Neat hedges will need annual trimming in June or July.

Propagation is by half ripe cuttings in August/September with a heel rooted in sandy compost in frames.

Genista lydia

HAMAMELIS

Hamamelis mollis

HAMAMELIS

The sweet-smelling "Witch Hazels" are quite rightly among the most popular garden plants. Their bright yellow flowers open from late December right through to March in cold winters and are followed by green leaves which turn yellow and red before they fall in autumn.

There are two main species, *Hamamelis japonica*, the "Japanese Witch Hazel" and the more widely grown *H. mollis* AGM, the "Chinese Witch Hazel". A cross between the two *H. x intermedia* has brought a number of excellent cultivars including: *H. x i.* 'Diane' AGM with copper red flowers and red autumn leaf colour; *H. x i* 'Jelena' AGM a large vigorous shrub with petals from yellow to copper red: and *H. x i.* 'Pallida' AGM, sweetly scented light yellow flowers make this one of the most popular of all.

Well worth seeking out for the purplish young leaves which turn green and then flame is *H. vernalis* 'Sandra' AGM, a cultivar of the "Ozark Witch Hazel" with heavily scented flowers in January and February.

HEATHS and HEATHERS

There are few plants which better supply colour the year round and easy work-free gardening once established than heaths and heathers. The name "Heather" commonly refers to three different genera used in this way, namely *Calluna, Daboecia* and *Erica*. To be pedantic the name "Heath" should refer to *Erica* and "Heather" or "Ling" to *Calluna*, the latter having broader, softer foliage.

While some of the winter-flowering heaths will grow in slightly alkaline soils, all the *Calluna* must have acid conditions. *Daboecia*, the "Irish", "Connemarra" or "St Dabeoc's Heath" have the largest flowers – up to half an inch long they hang like bells from May to late autumn.

There are so many cultivars it is difficult to cover them comprehensively here, suffice to say a selection should be made to provide a variety of leaf colours and different flowering times for maximum year-round impact. Among the late winter/early spring flowering types *Erica* x

Tip
Plant heathers in bold groups of at least 3–5 of each cultivar to get the best effect.

Hamamelis x intermedia 'Jelena'

Hamamelis x intermedia 'Pallida'

Daboecia

darleyensis 'Kramers Red' AGM and *E.* x *d.* 'Silberschmelze', a fragrant white are especially recommended.

Breeders are continually introducing improvements so *Calluna vulgaris* 'H.E. Beale", very popular bright pink late summer to early autumn flowering is now superseded by *C.v.* 'Annemarie' AGM growing to 50cm high. *C.v.* 'Robert Chapman' AGM is an excellent example of good leaf colour, starting golden in spring then turning orange to red in the winter. A watch should also be kept

Cultivation

Full sun is needed for the coloured-leaved forms especially. The *Erica carnea* cultivars grown for flowers will take some shade. While some winter-flowering heaths are lime-tolerant they all grow better in acid soils heavily enriched with well moistened sphagnum peat or leaf mould – especially acid pine-needle and bracken-leaf moulds.

Where soils are alkaline, flowers of sulphur at 100gm per square metre reduces the pH (acidity measure – 6.5pH = neutral) by one point. Watering with acidic fertilisers in spring will green up yellowing leaves caused by lack of iron.

Growth will be more compact with a light clip over after flowering. They are propagated from cuttings 3–5cm long taken July to October, pushed for two thirds their length into peat and sand and covered with polythene in a frame. The root-borne disease *Phytophthera* if introduced on diseased plants spreads quickly in hot weather and damp soils. Infected plants should be dug out and burnt and surrounding soil removed.

for the "Bud Bloomers", autumn flowering types which develop buds which never open, so provide good bud colour for weeks, most having girls' names of which *C.v.* 'Alexandra' , deep pink, is an example

If you are planting for long life – 15–20 years – choose *C. vulgaris* to 0.5m, *E. arborea* 1.5–2.5m, *E. carnea* 30cm, *E. erigena* 80cm and *E. vagans* to 1.3m.

Tip

The winter flowering Ericas are excellent tub plants. Combine with *senecio*, *skimmia* and *euonymus* for an interesting range of heights, leaf shapes and colours.

Erica carnea

Calluna vulgaris

HEBE

HEBE

The neat and compact forms of *Hebe* are very useful garden plants for tubs, window boxes and ground cover. Most species come from New Zealand and were previously called *Veronica*, now their common name. They provide shiny evergreen leaves and white flowers while many of the garden hybrids have coloured spikes of flower. As a general rule the smaller-leaved kinds are hardy while some of the larger-leaved and larger-flowered cultivars are killed by hard frost.

Good hardy small-leaved kinds for low shrub and ground cover use are: *H.* 'White Gem' to 1.5m; *H.* 'Carl Teschner' (syn. *H.* 'Youngii') 25cm, deep blue flowers; *H.* 'Margret' compact, eventually 45cm, rich green leaves and pale blue flowers; *H. pinguifolia* 'Pagei' AGM, 30cm, glaucous blue leaves, white flowers; and *H. pimeleoides* 'Quicksilver' AGM 45cm, near-black stems contrasting with silver leaves and blue-purple flowers.

Among the larger-leaved kinds *H.* x *franciscana* 'Variegata' AGM, to 1m has creamy white variegated leaves and lavender blue flowers, an

Hebe pinguifolia 'Pagei'

Hebe 'Midsummer Beauty'

excellent tub and window box plant when young; *H.* 'Midsummer Beauty' AGM, green with reddish underside to the leaf and lavender flowers; and *H.* 'Purple Queen', 120 cm, deep purple flowers and glossy dark leaves. One of the best garden pink-flowering hebes is 'Rosie' which flowers freely for weeks in summer.

Cultivation
Hebes prefer an open sunny site and light, well-drained soil. Many will prove hardier in poor soils, including chalk.

Young plants respond well to hard pruning in spring while old plants may die back.

Soft cuttings root easily and it is well worth taking a few each summer to provide replacements in the event of a hard winter.

HEDERA

The many different cultivars of ivy perform so many useful functions in gardens they deserve a book to themselves. Ideal for containers, for ground cover, to deck walls and fences and even on wire netting to form a neat hedge.

There are two common large-leaved species, *Hedera canariensis* being less hardy than *H. colchica* AGM, the "Persian Ivy".

Two good variegated forms are *H.c.* 'Dentata Variegata' AGM, creamy-yellow and green and *H.co.* 'Sulphur Heart' AGM (syn. *H.c.* 'Paddy's Pride') splashed yellow and dark green.

All the small-leaved *Hedera helix*, "Common Ivy", are reliably hardy. Popular garden cultivars include *H.h.* 'Goldheart' dark green and yellow; *H.h.* 'Glacier' AGM white, silver and grey-green; and *H.h.* 'Kolibri" AGM dark green blotched white.

Hedera helix 'Gold Heart'

Hedera canariensis 'Gloire de Marengo'

HIBISCUS

The "nurseryman"s nightmare" could well be the common name for *Hibiscus syriacus*, the "Tree Holly-hock", one of our most free-flowering shrubs of late summer. A nightmare because it is so late into leaf that new gardeners think it has died in spring.

There are both single and double cultivars, four good ones being *H.s.* 'Blue Bird'; *H.s.* 'Hamabo' AGM, blush pink and scarlet; *H.s.* 'Red Heart' AGM, white with bright red eye; and *H.s.* 'Woodbridge' AGM, rose pink; all fine plants in mixed borders and as single specimen plants.

Hibiscus syriacus 'Blue Bird'

HIPPOPHAE

The "Sea Buckthorn", *Hippophae rhamnoides* AGM is an easy to grow, vigorous shrub reaching 5m in height. It has slender silver-grey leaves and masses of orange berries – rich in vitamin C – on female plants.

Cultivation

Hippophae is a good coastal plant and an excellent screen against strong winds. It survives drought and sandy soils but also grows well in all garden soils, even those on the wet side.

Sow ripe seed in frames in October and trim hedges in August.

Hippophae rhamnoides

Tip

Ivy grow in full sun and shade, clad upright surfaces perfectly and, interplanted with large-flowered clematis, make the ideal partnership for north-facing walls.

Cultivation

All soils are suitable for *hedera* but when fed well in spring the new leaves have a much higher gloss.

Prune back in spring to retain size and rejuvenate the appearance.

Soft tip cuttings root easily virtually year-round under glass.

Cultivation

Hibiscus require full sun and a free-draining soil, given this most garden soils are suitable. In cold northern gardens they need the protection of a south-facing fence or wall.

No pruning is necessary but if hard pruned in spring and the new growth restricted to four or five branches, larger flowers will be produced.

They are fairly easy to root from half-ripe cuttings in sandy compost in July/August in frames. Flower bud browning and premature drop are likely in cold conditions and where the soil is dry and lacks fertiliser.

HYDRANGEA

HYDRANGEA

Many of the *Hydrangea macrophylla* cultivars are raised to be forced under glass and sold as flowering pot plants. These do not, however, always prove the best garden plants.

Careful selection of well-proven garden cultivars will give massed floral displays for many weeks. There are other good garden species too such as *Hydrangea arborescens* 'Annabelle' AGM, a loose plant of suckering habit to 1.5m in height and spread and huge rounded heads of white sterile flowers.

Most reliable of all is *H. paniculata* 'Grandiflora' AGM, a large shrub growing to 3m with showy conical heads of white flowers in August that turn antique pink and then brown as they age. Hard pruning each spring produces tall branches with huge flower heads, so large they may need support in heavy rain. *H.p.* 'Kyushu' AGM is a compact form with a mixture of large sterile and small frilly fertile flowers and *H.p.* 'Praecox' AGM is an earlier-flowering form.

While *H. petiolaris* is a climbing plant, ideal for north walls, it can also

Cultivation

All hydrangeas are excellent plants to use as single specimens, grouped in loose hedges, on banks and in mixed borders. They grow particularly well in mild coastal areas with good rainfall.

The hortensias make excellent pot and patio tub plants.

Most are hungry feeders and need free-draining soils in winter and masses of water in summer. Spring planting is advisable so that the tender types can get well established before winter cold.

Little pruning is necessary save the thinning out of old wood either in spring or immediately after flowering for early flowering "Mop Heads".

Propagate from soft cuttings in summer. Spray to control aphids and to keep them free of vine weevil.

The only special treatment is for plants with yellowing leaves, these need iron sequestrene in April.

be grown as a free-standing shrub. In its native Japan it can reach 20m and more, climbing tree trunks. Old stems have interesting peeling bark and well-established plants produce large flower heads with white sterile flowers around the outer edge and dull white fertile flowers within in June. If a container plant can be bought in bud or flower this precocious flowering is likely to continue.

The "Oak-leaved Hydrangea", *H. quercifolia* has deeply-scalloped green leaves that, like most of this genera, colour in the autumn with broad white conical flowers in August/September that turn purplish-pink and then brown with age. This needs a sheltered warm site and reaches 1.5m.

Good garden kinds of *H. macrophylla* include: the "Mop Head" or "Hortensias": – *H.m.* 'Alpen Glow' with bright red flowers from July to November, recovers from spring frost damage to bloom in the autumn; *H.m.* 'Altona' AGM, cherry-pink or blue; *H.m.* 'Madame Emile Mouillere' AGM is a popular white to 1.2m with pink or blue eye, very free-flowering but needing a warm site.

Next but equally beautiful are the "Lace-caps" with outer ring of large sterile "ray florets" and centre of tiny florets that look like those lace caps worn by maids in Victorian times. *H.m.* 'Blue Wave' AGM, deep blue or rose pink; *H.m.* 'Mariesii', pink or mauve-pink and pale blue in acid soils; *H.m.* 'Geoffrey Chadbund" AGM brick red on compact growth to 1–2m. Where two colours are listed for one cultivar this is because in acid soils that contain aluminium many red- or pink-flowered forms turn blue or mauve. As a general rule all whites remain white whatever the soil, some reds and pinks turn blue or mauve in acid soils. Flower colour is somewhat unpredictable and deep blues are only achieved in acid soils. In mildy alkaline soils aluminium sulphate at 0.5–1kg (1–2lb) per large shrub will

Hydrangea macrophylla

Hydrangea petiolaris

turn some reds and pinks blue.

H. *serrata* 'Preziosa' AGM is a handsome, long-flowering plant with purplish stems, purple-tinged young leaves and rose-pink flowers that deepen as the autumn advances. H. *aspera* 'Villosa Group' AGM is a lovely later-flowering shrub – August/September – reaching 2m with large lilac-blue flowers. The leaves are soft, deep green, bristly above and grey beneath, it grows in chalk and can survive dry soils but needs protection as a young plant.

HYPERICUM

Large yellow buttercup-like flowers are produced by all these shrubs, which range from ground-coverers to head-high types. The British native *Hypericum androsaemum* will survive shade and grows to 1m, the small light yellow flowers opening from June to September and followed by red berry-like seed heads.

"Rose of Sharon" or "St John's Wort", H. *calycinum* is an excellent ground coverer, almost evergreen – the leaves falling in hard winter frost – and reaching 0.3m. A rapidly spreading plant even in dry soil and dense shade, it is ideal for banks, under trees and anywhere dark green leaf cover and weed smothering is required. The leaves are covered in golden yellow flowers 7cm across from June to September.

Hypericum forrestii AGM forms an upright shrub to just over 1m, yellow flowers in summer and autumn being followed by attractive foliage colour before leaves fall. H. 'Hidcote' AGM is a superb garden and landscape shrub, semi-evergreen and eventually reaching 2m, it forms a semi-globe shape of bright yellow flowers from July to October. It grows well in sun and part shade and should be in every mixed shrub border.

H. x *inodorum* 'Elstead' grows to 2m and has small yellow flowers from July to October followed by stunning salmon-red fruits, the leaves turning purplish before they fall. H. x *moserianum* AGM grows to 0.5m to form a rounded shrub and H. x m. 'Tricolour' is not so hardy and has pink, cream and green foliage. H. 'Rowallane' AGM is often said to be better than H. 'Hidcote' but is not as hardy.

Cultivation

Hypericum are suitable for all soils including chalk. They grow in sun and shade although flower better in sun. Avoid heavy water-logged clay.

Prune occasionally in spring to remove some old wood except H. *calycinum* and H. x *inodorum* which can be pruned hard back in March.

They root easily from half-ripe cuttings in frames in May/June.

Rust disease can be a problem with H. *calycinum* and H. x *i.* 'Elstead'. Systemic fungicide sprays will contain this.

Hydrangea macrophylla

Hypericum calycinum

ILEX

The evergreen "Common Holly", *Ilex aquifolium* AGM with its prickly dark evergreen leaves and bright red fruits is as useful in the garden year-round as it is popular for its seasonal Christmas berries. There are over 300 species and cultivars, many of them excellent garden plants but most having either male or female flowers.

This is confusingly illustrated by *Ilex aquifolium* 'Silver Queen' AGM (a male) with white-margined leaves and no fruit and *I.* x *altaclarensis* 'Golden King' AGM (female) with golden, almost spineless, variegated leaves and good red berries. Three widely-planted self-fertile cultivars are the almost spineless *I.a.* 'J. C. Van Tol', *I.a.* 'Pyramidalis' AGM with rich dark green leaves and heavy crops of berries, even on young plants and *I.a.* 'Madame Briot'.

Other popular cultivars include: *I.a.* 'Handsworth New Silver' AGM, a female with purple stems and leaves

Ilex aquifolium 'J.C. van Tol'

edged cream, *I.a.* 'Ferox', the "Hedgehog Holly" so named because of the fiercely-thorned leaves and *I.a.* 'Ferox Argentea' AGM with white margin to the leaf (both male) and *I. a.* 'Silver Milkmaid' AGM with centre of the leaf blotched deep cream.

So called "Blue Hollies", *Ilex x meserveae* bred by Eileen Meserve in Long Island, New York have dark, almost metallic black shiny mature leaves and are very hardy. *I. x m.* 'Blue

Angel' AGM and *I. x m.* 'Blue Princess' are good females and *I. x m.* 'Blue Prince' is a stronger-growing male for cross-pollination to 3m.

All are good plants to grow in mixed borders, as hedges, in pots and to stand as specimens in grass. Most make tall shrubs to small trees. Grow *Kerria* among the taller ones and have yellow flowers in spring.

Cultivation

Hollies grow well in all soils, in sun and shade, withstanding city grime and coastal wind, but they do not transplant easily so use pot-grown plants.

You can prune all of these hard back – usually for Christmas foliage – and they soon grow away again.

The best hedge trimming time is July, with hard pruning to retain size in April.

Propagation is by cuttings with a heel from August to October, rooted in frames.

Ilex aquifolium 'Handsworth New Silver'

Ilex aquifolium 'Madame Briot'

Ilex meserveae 'Blue Princess'

INDIGOFERA

There is a special elegance to the loose spreading habit of *Indigofera heterantha* AGM (syn. *I. gerardiana*), late into leaf, its pea-shaped rose-purple flowers developing on the tips of branches from July to October.

It is not completely hardy and requires the protection of a south-facing wall where it will grow taller, to 3m. Should frost cut the stems back they usually break again from the base.

Indigofera heterantha

Cultivation
Both acid and alkaline soils are suitable for *Indigofera* and a warm, free-draining site is best.

Plants can be pruned hard back in spring like fuchsias and propagation is by seed and half-ripe cuttings in frames in summer.

JASMINUM

Jasminum officinale

JASMINUM
Probably the best known and most widely planted free-flowering winter shrub is *Jasminum nudiflorum* AGM, "Winter-flowering Jasmine". The leafless green stems provide flush after flush of scentless yellow blooms through the winter. It is generally grown against fences and walls in all sorts of soil. It can also be grown free-standing to form a low hummocky

Jasminum nudiflorum

bush and at the top of banks to cascade down. Side branches can be pruned immediately after flowering to stimulate new flowering side shoots to flower the following season.

J. humile 'Revolutum' AGM, "Himalayan Jasmine" is an evergreen non-twining shrub with slightly fragrant yellow flowers from June to August. It grows to 2m in height and 1.6m spread and is best against a south- or west-facing wall.

J. officinale AGM the "Common White Jasmine" is a rampant twining deciduous climber to 10m with very fragrant white flowers. In rich soils the flowers are sparse and can be lost in the foliage so it is best against a wall or tree where moisture is limited in summer. *J.o.* 'Fiona Sunrise' has yellow foliage which deepens in autumn.

J. x stephanense AGM is a semi-evergreen climber to 6m with fragrant pale pink flowers in June. It needs space and would help to hide a shed. The foliage on new shoots is often flushed cream.

J. polyanthum AGM is a very popular houseplant with sweetly scented, pink in bud, white flowers. While it makes a good conservatory plant it is not hardy although can survive outside in warm city centres such as London and Bournemouth. Restrict watering in July/August to encourage this species to form flower bud.

Cultivation
Any well-drained soil is suitable for the Jasmines. No regular pruning is needed, just thinning out of some old stems now and again.

In August/September propagate from half-ripe cuttings in frames or cover stems at this time with soil to produce layers in one year.

KALMIA
The Kalmias are evergreen shrubs, close relatives of rhododendrons and liking similar although rather sunnier conditions. Flowering later in June, they bring useful pink and red colour at that time.

Kalmia angustifolia AGM is a low shrub to 1m commonly called "Sheep Laurel" because it and other Kalmias are poisonous to animals.

Best known is *K. latifolia* AGM, the "Calico Bush" reaching 3m in Britain and up to 9m in its native N. America. *K.l.* 'Ostbo Red' AGM has red rather than pink-coloured flowers.

Cultivation
Kalmias require moist acid soils and transplant well in September/ October and March/April.

No pruning is necessary save the removal of dying flowers and propagation is by seed, cuttings and, probably best for gardeners, layers.

KERRIA
A suckering green-stemmed shrub to 2m, *Kerria japonica* is one of the easiest shrubs to grow and produces bright yellow flowers in April/May.

Commonly called "Jew's Mallow", *K.j.* 'Pleniflora' AGM has double flowers and grows a little taller while *K.j.* 'Variegata' (syn. *K.j.* 'Picta') has creamy-white variegated leaves. Plant kerria alongside a well established holly and it will grow through the holly branches to 4m. Yellow flowers show up against the dark green holly.

Cultivation
Old *Kerria* shrubs can have old stems thinned out after flowering.

Propagate by digging up suckers in autumn and by means of half-ripe cuttings August/September

KOLKWITZIA

Commonly called "Beauty Bush" in the States, *Kolkwitzia amabilis* has masses of pale pink foxglove-like flowers in May/June. *K.a.* 'Pink Cloud' AGM, raised in 1946 at Wisley Gardens, has deeper pink flowers on a dense, well-branched plant. Can eventually grow to 3m in height.

Kalmia latifolia

Kolkwitzia amabilis

Cultivation

All soils are suitable for *Kolkwitzia* including chalk, ideally choose a sunny and free-draining site.

Pruning is no more than the cutting out of some old branches after flowering.

Propagation of named cultivars is by cuttings in July/August in frames.

Kerria japonica 'Pleniflora'

LAURUS

LAURUS

The "Tree Laurel" *Laurus nobilis* AGM, used by the Romans to adorn the brows of heroes and, when berried, the brows of poets – as in "poet laureate" – is more commonly called "Sweet Bay" and "Bay Laurel".

An attractive evergreen, perhaps better known to cooks than gardeners. There is a golden form *L.n.* 'Aurea' AGM which is most attractive in winter and spring.

They grow 4–6m high in sheltered sites and as single specimens grow into an appealing conical shape. Bay can also be used as a hedge in warm and coastal areas and grows very well in containers if given protection from hard winter frost.

Laurus nobilis

LAVANDULA

"Old English Lavender", *Lavandula angustifolia* AGM or one of its cultivars should be in every garden. Few plants have so many qualities and none can rival its fragrance.

L.a. 'Alba' is a strong upright form growing to 1m high with white flowers from July; *L.a.* 'Nana Alba' is compact to 0.3m; *L.a.* 'Hidcote' AGM is one of the best, with compact narrow growth to 0.6m and dense flower spikes of deep violet that need to be crushed to release their fragrance; *L.a.* 'Lodden Pink" grows to 0.7m and has rather insipid pink flowers from early July; *L.a.* 'Twickel Purple' AGM is compact, has broader leaves and fragrant flowers; and *L.a.* 'Munstead', to 0.7m, has the bluest flowers, from late July.

L. x *intermedia* 'Dutch Group' AGM (syn. *L.* 'Vera') commonly called "Dutch Lavender" has broad silver-grey leaves and lavender flowers from late July on plants 1–1.2m high.

"French Lavender",: *L. stoechas* AGM requires a warmer site to grow well to 0.6m. The tuft of purple bracts on the top of each flower has been described as pineapple-like and appears from May to July.

Unless otherwise stated they have grey-green leaves year-round and are especially attractive as young plants in winter. Lavenders are useful to the front of mixed borders, among hardy border flowers and as low hedges. Planted close they provide ground cover for several years.

Lavandula angustifolia

Lavatera 'Rosea'

Lavatera 'Barnsley'

LAVATERA

Warm summers and mild winters in the 1988–96 period saw *Lavatera* rocket in popularity. *L.* 'Barnsley' AGM, white flowers with red centre, can revert to the rose pink of *L.* 'Rosea' AGM, which grows to 2m. *L.* 'Burgundy Wine' is a more compact shrub with purple flowers.

Cultivation

All soils are suitable, especially light chalky ones and *Lavatera* thrives in coastal areas.

They are not completely hardy and it is advisable to take new cuttings each summer, when they root easily.

Straggly branches can be pruned right back in spring, which delays flowering by two or three weeks and gives much more shapely growth.

LEYCESTERIA

Used mainly for its novelty value as a garden plant, *Leycesteria formosa* has many common names including "Japanese Lantern" and "Granny's Curls", which refer to the claret bracts and white flowers. These are followed by purple berries eaten by game birds.

A useful plant in woodland and large gardens but can be a little too vigorous in small plots.

Cultivation

All soils are suitable and self-sown seedlings spread by birds often occur in gardens. Hard frost may damage branches but the plant soon grows again from the base.

Prune out old stems in March.

Propagate by sowing fresh seed in the autumn and by softwood cuttings in summer.

Leycesteria formosa

LIGUSTRUM

LIGUSTRUM

The rich green, either yellow- or cream-and-green forms of *Ligustrum*, commonly called "Privet" are among the most widely planted of all shrubs, especially for hedges.

Easiest of all is *Ligustrum ovalifolium*, the green-leaved privet reaching 6m unpruned. More attractive and less vigorous are *L.o.* 'Argenteum' with leaves edged creamy-white and less vigorous again, *L.o.* 'Aureum' AGM the "Golden Privet" with rich yellow leaves, especially on the young tips which develop green centres as they mature.

Quite a strong-growing shrub to 5m and more, *L. quihoui* AGM produces big clusters of white flowers on the tips of branches in August and September. *L.* 'Vicaryi' has bold yellow leaves which turn bronze in autumn.

Most will lose their leaves in harsh winter weather and become deciduous especially on impoverished

Ligsutrum ovalifolium 'Aureum'

Cultivation

These adaptable plants grow in a very wide variety of soils and almost any position, even dense shade, wet heavy land and under the drip of trees.

Where any form grows too strongly or where the job of trimming hedges becomes too arduous, the rate of growth can be controlled by spraying with dikegulac (Cutlass) after trimming in May.

When planting new privet hedges it is well worth cutting the growth back by half in early spring to encourage plenty of strong basal growth. Over-sized plants respond well to cutting really hard back at pretty well any time although early spring, when the new growth soon covers the cuts, is best.

Ligustrum propagates easily from either soft young shoots rooted under glass in summer or, more commonly, from hardwood cuttings 30–37cm long taken late autumn. Remove lower leaves and insert for half their length in sandy soil.

soils. All respond well to clipping and are commonly used for topiary work as well as for hedges in all sizes.

The erect clusters of white summer flowers have a rather heavy, insipid if not unpleasant smell and some set black berries which are eaten by birds. Ingestion of all parts of these plants should be avoided by humans.

No flower arranger's garden should be without some "Golden Privet", a good source of attractive foliage.

They grow well in mixed shrub borders, suit container growing, especially in the coloured-leaved forms as well as spaced 0.3–0.5m apart for hedging.

Ligustrum ovalifolium

Lonicera periclymenum

LONICERA – Climbing

The "Woodbine", our common hedgerow honeysuckle, *Lonicera periclymenum* has a sweet and fresh fragrance all its own. No garden, especially country garden, should be without the pale yellow flowers which open in July and August to be followed by translucent scarlet berries.

Good cultivars include: *L.p.* 'Belgica' AGM the "Early Dutch Honeysuckle"; *L.p.* 'Graham Thomas' AGM a very long-flowering form: *L.p.* 'Harlequin' with variegated leaves and pink and cream flowers; *L.p.* 'Serotina' AGM the "Late Dutch Honeysuckle"; all twining up 5–6m and more high.

Grown in pots and the young shoots repeatedly trimmed, they form rounded free-flowering shrubs. *L. serotina* 'Honeybush' is a shrubby form – its occasional long stem should be pruned back to retain the compact habit.

Other useful species are *L. x americana* AGM, fragrant white flowers coloured pink to red on the tube; *L. x brownii* 'Dropmore Scarlet', orange-red tubular flowers from late May to August and occasionally to October; *L. x heckrottii* 'Goldflame', orange to yellow flowers from June to September; *L. japonica* 'Halliana'

AGM is nearly evergreen the leaves often hiding the white to cream flowers, nicely scented; and *L. x tellmanniana* AGM has long golden yellow flowers from early to mid summer.

These climbing types have many uses and grow well up walls, over fences and pergolas as well as up through big shrubs and trees. When planted against trees water well in dry weather and feed regularly to support both lots of roots.

Cultivation

Rich, damp soils and shade at the root suits the climbing honeysuckles. Partial shade suits them well and they will flower in shade. Pruning is no more than the occasional removal of old wood immediately after flowering.

Cuttings taken in July/August of 10cm long soft to half ripe pieces of stem root fairly easily in frames and under polythene.

Spray to control aphids, a common summer pest which in severe attacks prevents flowering. Sticky exudation from aphids encourages black sooty mould fungus.

Tip

Use *Lonicera japonica* 'Aureoreticulata' in flower arrangements. It has attractive golden veining to the leaves which provide good contrast to cut blooms. The curling tips of young shoots are especially attractive in table decorations.

Lonicera japonica 'Aureoreticulata'

Lonicera x heckrottii 'Goldflame'

Lonicera japonica 'Halliana'

Lonicera x brownii 'Dropmore Scarlet'

LONICERA – Shrubby

There are a number of shrubby honeysuckles that make very useful garden plants. Best known is *Lonicera nitida*, clothed in small evergreen leaves and widely used as a low- to medium-sized hedge. They need clipping several times a year to retain a neat shape and if more than 1m high may need a support wire through the centre.

L.n. 'Baggesen's Gold' AGM is an attractive golden-leaved form used as a free-standing shrub in mixed borders. This needs full sun for the brightest colour. *L.n.* 'Maigrun' ('Maygreen') is a compact plant with shiny green leaves which stay on the plant longer in cold weather; and *L.n.* 'Silver Beauty' has an eye-catching silver edge to the leaf.

Both gold- and silver-edged leaf forms make good window box and patio pot fillers in young plant size.

L. fragrantissima is partially evergreen to 2m and has cream-coloured scented flowers in the winter. It can be rather shy flowering out in the open and blooms better against a south or west facing wall. *L. standishii* is more compact and flowers more freely than *fragrantissima* and produces red berries. A cross between *L.f.* and *L.s.* gave *L.* x *purpusii*, a deciduous shrub reaching 2m and more with very sweetly scented flowers in winter.

Easiest of all is *L. tatarica*, a vigorous shrub to 3m with pale pink flowers on the tips of branches in May/June.

Tip

Use *Lonicera pileata* for good ground covering. It reaches 1.5m and has large, almost box-like leaves. It is also good planted on banks and beneath trees.

Lonicera tatarica

Cultivation

All soils and sites are suitable for these shrubs, *Lonicera nitida* for hedging should be planted 0.3m apart and pruned back by half to build up a well-branched base.

Free-standing shrubs need no more than a few old branches pruned out after flowering.

Propagate from hardwood cuttings pushed into sandy soil in the autumn.

Lonicera nitida 'Baggesen's Gold'

MAGNOLIA

MAGNOLIA

Most people are familiar with the dramatic spring flowering Magnolias, shrubs and small trees with large upright tulip-like flowers. Most common are forms of *Magnolia* x *soulangeana* which produce lots of showy white flowers overlaid wine-purple on the outside of the blooms on leafless branches in April.

Good cultivars are: M. x s. 'Lennei' AGM with huge rose-purple flowers; and its ivory white form M. x s. 'Lennei Alba' AGM; M. x s. 'Picture', similar to the type but young plants flower sooner; and M. x s. 'Rustica Rubra' AGM with rich rosy red flowers.

One of the parents of M. x *soulangeana*, M. *liliiflora* is especially suited to the smaller garden, reaching only 3.5m in height. Erect flowers open between late April and June and often continue throughout the summer. Even more compact in growth and with slightly larger flowers, *M.l.* 'Nigra' AGM is deep purple in colour.

A real garden gem is the "Star Magnolia", M. *stellata* which grows slowly to an eventual height of 2–3m. It is covered with masses of star-like fragrant white blooms in March to April. M.s. 'Rosea' has pink-flushed flowers and M.s. 'Water Lily' AGM has larger flowers with more tepals (a combination of sepal and petal which occurs on these shrubs).

All the spring-flowering forms are best planted where their blooms are protected from cold winds and rapid thawing in early morning sunshine after overnight frost, both of which cause the tepals to become bruised and brown.

Summer-flowering M. *sieboldii* AGM is less well known, perhaps because the pendant cup-shaped flowers hang down among the leaves.

Magnolia liliiflora 'Nigra'

They are pleasantly lemon-scented and have crimson stamens in a ring contrasting with the pearly-white flowers, which are very photogenic. These flowers are followed by pink fruits that open in October to expose the orange seeds.

Magnolia grandiflora is by contrast a large evergreen tree, growing 5–7m high and 5m or more across with large laurel-like leaves, glossy green above and reddish-brown and felted beneath. Its large, strongly lemon-scented flowers 20cm or more across

Magnolia sieboldii

Magnolia grandiflora

Magnolia stellata

appear from July to September. While usually planted against a wall it is hardy in the open in warmer parts of Britain. M.g. 'Exmouth' AGM is an excellent form with paler green leaves and huge flowers 25cm across which form on quite young plants; and M.g. 'Goliath' AGM is another large-flowered form.

Cultivation

Many magnolias are lime-haters and are best in reasonably rich deep soil. Provided that drainage is good they will tolerate heavy clay and withstand the dirt of towns and cities.

Warm, sheltered sites and soils well supplied with organic material in the form of leaf mould or peat will give the best growth. A little extra attention at the outset to get young plants established will be rewarded by many years of exotic flowers.

Container-grown plants with roots very well established in their pots are much easier to establish than lifted and root-balled or containerised specimens.

They need no pruning but unwanted branches are best pruned off completely immediately after flowering.

Propagate by layering in March/April, a slow but sure process which can take two years.

The popular deciduous magnolias make excellent tub plants.

Magnolia soulangeana

MAHONIA

MAHONIA

There are two clear groups of *Mahonia*, the spring-flowering M. *aquifolium* types and the winter-flowering kinds. Both have attractive evergreen leaves. Commonly called "Oregon Grape", M. *aquifolium* has yellow flowers in March and April followed by purplish-blue berries loved by blackbirds. The leaves are a shiny dark green, turning bronze and purple in winter, on branches 1–1.2m height.

M.*a.* 'Apollo' AGM is a large-flowered form and M.*a.* 'Smaragd' has bronze young leaves that mature to a rich green. Where a taller, more upright plant is required choose M. x *wagneri* 'Pinnacle' AGM (the name M. *pinnata* has been incorrectly attributed to this). The aquifoliums are suckering and make good ground cover.

M. *japonica* AGM has deep green leaves with 7–17 leaflets, grows to 3m and has fragrant yellow flowers from mid-winter to early spring. M. x *media* comes from M. *japonica* crossed with the larger, upright-flowering and not so hardy M. *lomariifolia* AGM, flowering from late autumn to mid-winter and slightly fragrant. Good garden forms are M. x *m.* 'Buckland' AGM with good autumn leaf colour; M. x *m* 'Charity' AGM with leaves up to 50cm long; M. x *m.* 'Lionel Fortescue' with masses of fragrant flowers; and M. x *m* 'Winter Sun" AGM of medium size, with flower heads packed with fragrant blooms.

Mahonia aquifolium 'Apollo'

Cultivation

Mahonias are not fussy over soil, even some chalk, but produce the best foliage in soils improved with leaf mould and peat.

All withstand shade and respond well to pruning hard back when necessary and then immediately after flowering.

Propagation of *Mahonia aquifolium* is by division and from 7.5cm cuttings in July. The large-leaved winter-flowering kinds are not so easy and best rooted as leaf bud cuttings on mist benches under glass in summer.

Mahonia x media 'Charity'

Mahonia japonica 'Bealei Group'

MYRTUS

The "Common Myrtle", *Myrtus communis* AGM is a leafy evergreen reaching 3–4m in sheltered gardens. White flowers open from July to September, are followed by purple fruits and the leaves have a spicy fragrance when crushed. *M. communis tarentina* AGM (syn. M.c. 'Nana' has pink tinted cream flowers and white berries.

Myrtus communis tarentina

Cultivation

Myrtus grow well in any well-drained soil, including chalk and seaside sites but are best used as wall shrubs and conservatory plants in most parts of Britain.

They require a long hot summer to encourage free flowering.

They need little pruning save the removal in spring of branches damaged by frost.

Propagate by cuttings taken with a heel in June/July and rooted in a heated frame.

OLEARIA

Three evergreen species make useful garden shrubs. *Olearia* x *macrodonta* AGM, the "New Zealand Holly", grows to 4m, has sage-green leaves and clusters of white flowers in June. *O.* x *haastii* grows eventually to 2m with smaller oval leaves and clusters of hawthorn-scented flowers in July and August. *O.* x *scilloniensis* (syn. *O. stellulata* 'De Candolle' AGM) grows to 1.5m, the small grey leaves disappearing under white flowers in May/June.

Olearia x macrodonta

Cultivation

All *Olearia* are good seaside plants, growing well in free-draining and chalky soils, preferably in a sunny position. If cut down by frost they usually break again from the base.

Dead flower heads can look untidy and are easily cleared by shearing over after flowering. Any other thinning and shaping is best done in April.

Propagate by means of half-ripe cuttings in frames in August.

OSMANTHUS

Rich dark evergreen leaves and fragrant white flowers in April are provided by *Osmanthus delavayi* AGM and *O.* x *burkwoodii* AGM, spreading shrubs eventually reaching 2.5–3m and best given south wall protection in cold areas.

O. heterophyllus is a slow-growing holly-like shrub easily distinguished from holly by its leaves which are opposite up the stem, not in pairs. Tiny fragrant flowers open in clusters in September and October. There are several variegated-leaved forms such as *O.h.* 'Variegatus' AGM which make good container plants.

Cultivation

All good soils are suitable for *Osmanthus* in sun and shade. Little pruning is necessary and any trimming can be done in April.

Propagate from half-ripe cuttings in frames in July.

Osmanthus delavayi

Osmanthus heterophyllus 'Variegatus'

PAEONIA – Tree Paeony

PAEONIA – Tree Paeony

It is difficult to imagine more spectacular flowers than cultivars of the "Tree Paeony", *Paeonia suffruticosa*, which open 15–20cm across in April and May on plants up to 2m in size. Their large compound leaves are also attractive and take on autumn tints before they fall.

In spring the tender shoots are susceptible to late frost, otherwise they are completely hardy.

Paeonia suffruticosa

Cultivation

Most plants for sale have been grafted onto herbaceous *Paeonia lactiflora* and need to be planted so that the graft is covered by 6cm of soil to encourage the tree paeony to produce its own roots.

All the pruning needed is the removal of dead wood in March. Where plants get rather tall and leggy it is all right to prune back hard after flowering. The new shoots may take two years to flower.

PARTHENOCISSUS

Much confusion surrounds the names of these self-clinging vines, due perhaps to earlier references under the names *Ampelopsis* and *Vitis*. The confusion becomes greater with the common name "Virginia Creeper" often applied to the wrong plant.

The best known and most widely planted is *Parthenocissus tricuspidata* AGM, commonly called 'Boston Ivy' which has three-lobed leaves on mature plants. *P.t.* 'Veitchii' is a smaller-leaved form with young growth tinged purple.

The true "Virginia Creeper", *P. quinquefolia* AGM has more deeply cut and five-lobed leaves. *P. henryana* AGM has dark bronze-green leaves

Cultivation

Parthenocissus quinquefolia and Parthenocissus tricuspidata grow rapidly to 10m or more and should be pruned away from roofs and windows after leaf fall.

Acceptable growth is achieved in all soils, rich loamy soils giving prodigious wall and fence cover.

Propagate from half-ripe cuttings in August or September under polythene.

with each mid rib showing white or pink variegation when grown in shade.

All three turn rich crimson and scarlet before the leaves fall in autumn.

Parthenocissus tricuspidata 'Veitchii'

PEROVSKIA

Bright blue flower spikes in autumn and greyish-green leaves with the fragrance of sage are the qualities of *Perovskia atriplicifolia* AGM, commonly called "Russian Sage".

Cultivation

Perovskia grows 1.5m high and thrives in most soils including chalk, and in coastal areas.

Any sunny, well-drained soil is suitable and they are best treated like herbaceous plants, cutting back to 24cm in March.

Perovskia atriplicifolia

Pernettya mucronata

PERNETTYA

Dense, small evergreen-leaved growth up to 1m is provided by *Pernettya mucronata* AGM (now called *Gaultheria*). It carries male and female flowers on separate plants and you need one male, such as *P.m.* 'Thymifolia' to every four or five females to get good cross pollination and masses of bright berries in autumn and winter.

Good female cultivars include: *P.m.* 'Crimsonia' AGM, with large deep crimson berries; *P.m.* 'Lilian', pink fruits and *P.m.* 'Wintertime' AGM, white fruits. Male and female flowers grow on *P.m.* 'Bell's Seedling' AGM so this will self-set large dark red berries.

Cultivation

All *Pernettya* are lime haters and need to be grown in acid soils.

They prefer a partially shaded site and grow best where peaty compost has been mixed into the soil.

When they get too tall and rather leggy they can be "dropped" like heathers, that is lifted with a good ball of soil and planted much deeper, up to half their height being covered with soil. Branches will root out anew and some can then be cut off to propagate more plants.

Healthy old plants can be pruned back in late winter or early spring to get new growth.

PHILADELPHUS

PHILADELPHUS

Wafts of heady fragrance on a midsummer's evening are the hallmark of the white-flowering *Philadelphus*, commonly called "Mock Orange" because of the similarity of its scent to that of orange blossom.

Almost the perfect garden plant, being easy to grow, undemanding culturally, available in a range of varieties from 1–4m high and very free-flowering. By far the most popular is *P.* 'Virginal' (LA '82) AGM, which grows to 3m but is fairly upright, spreading little more than 2m. It has large double flowers 25cm across which are strongly scented and hang on the plant in clusters.

One of the best singles is *P.* 'Belle Etoile' AGM growing to 3m and with petal bases flushed purple; *P.* 'Beauclerk' AGM is smaller but with larger flowers. *P. coronarius* is medium sized has denser growth and yellowish

Cultivation

Any garden soil is suitable, *Philadelphus* thrive in the poorest conditions, including chalk. Free-draining soils are best and although they can be grown in partial shade flowering will be better in sunnier places.

Pruning consists of no more than the removal of a few old branches after flowering.

Propagation is by half-ripe cuttings in summer or, more easily, by hardwood cuttings outside in the autumn.

white flowers; while *P.c.* 'Aureus' AGM grows to 1m with bright yellow leaves that age to pale green.

Even more compact are *P.* 'Manteau d'Hermine' AGM, a very free-flowering creamy white; and *P. microphyllus* with small leaves and masses of sweetly-scented flowers.

PHOTINIA see also *Stranvaesia*

The evergreen *Photinia* x *fraseri* is the *Pieris* substitute for chalky soils. It has bright coppery-red young leaves on the tips of branches all summer that mature to glossy dark green. *P.* x *f.* 'Red Robin' AGM has toothed leaves and very bright young growth while *P.* x *f.* 'Robusta' AGM is the hardiest of current cultivars.

Cultivation

Choose a sheltered site for *Photinia*. Any pruning to shape plants and hedges should be done in early spring.

Propagate from half-ripe cuttings in frames in summer.

Photinia x fraseri 'Red Robin'

Philadelphus 'Virginal'

Physocarpus opulifolius 'Dart's Gold'

Pieris 'Forest Flame'

PHYSOCARPUS

An easy shrub which is grown for its colourful deciduous foliage. Reaching 1.5m *Physocarpus opulifolius* has bark which peels attractively. *P.o.* 'Dart's Gold' AGM has yellow leaves and *P.o.* 'Diabolo' is deep copper.

Cultivation
Most soils are suitable but *Physocarpus* prefer moist, heavier types in sun.

Prune a quarter of old stems out after flowering to stimulate new growth.

PIERIS

Attractive red shoots, evergreen leaves and white lily-of-the-valley-like flowers make *Pieris* lovely plants for gardens with acid soils.

You need milder gardens for *Pieris formosa* and it is well worth finding warm positions for *P.f.* 'Jermyns' AGM with deep red young leaves and masses of red flower buds and stems all winter opening to white flowers in spring and *P.f.* 'Wakehurst' AGM with very red young shoots and bright white flowers.

There are a number of lovely *P. japonica* cultivars with good evergreen foliage and fragrant flowers. *P.j.* 'Blush' AGM has coppery young leaves and deep pink flowers; *P.j.* 'Debutante' AGM is a low grower with white flowers loved by bumble bees. *P.j.* 'Pink Delight' AGM has

Cultivation
Similar to rhododendrons, *Pieris* require either lime-free soil or raised beds enriched with acid peat.

They grow best if not allowed to dry out in summer and a mulch in spring with peat or acid leaf mould helps to retain moisture (pine needles and oak leaves mixed is ideal).

The only pruning needed is the removal of dead flowers and any frost-damaged shoots.

Propagate by means of half-ripe cuttings in frames in August or layer low branches in September.

pale pink flowers; and *P.j.* 'Scarlett O'Hara' has dark red new shoots and white flowers.

One of the most popular garden plants is *P.* 'Forest Flame' AGM with young shoots that go from red through pink to cream and then green and masses of white flowers.

Tip
Where the soil is alkaline *Pieris* make good container plants but remember to use an ericaceous compost.

Pieris japonica 'Debutante'

PITTOSPORUM

PITTOSPORUM

A group of tender shrubs grown mostly for their evergreen foliage, for garden decoration and for cutting to use in arrangements. Grown commercially in the warm south west as a cut foliage crop for florists.

Upright branches to 4m and more are formed on *Pittosporum tenuifolium* AGM, the bark on young stems is dark grey to black, a good contrast to the bright shiny pale green leaves and small honey-scented purplish flowers which appear in late spring. They are followed by black berries. There are a number of attractive cultivars including: *P.t.* 'Irene Paterson' AGM with leaves opening cream, developing to green marbled white and maturing to pale green which gets a pink tinge in winter; *P.t.* 'Silver Queen' AGM; *P.t.* 'Tom Thumb' AGM, a dense rounded shrub, green to deep purple; and *P.t.* 'Warnham Gold' AGM maturing to golden yellow in autumn.

Tip

All the cultivars make good unheated conservatory plants to grow in pots and stand outside for the summer. When brought under glass in October water sparingly in cold conditions.

Cultivation

All well drained soils are suitable for *Pittosporum* and a sheltered position is essential in most of Britain. Hedge plants should be spaced 0.5m apart and any pruning is either undertaken in spring to remove frost-damaged shoots or in July to shape hedges.

Half-ripe cuttings can be rooted in July in a frame with bottom heat.

POLYGONUM

See *Fallopia baldschuanica*

Pittosporum tenuifolium 'Silver Queen'

POTENTILLA

There is no better group of plants for flower power than forms of the shrubby *Potentilla*, producing single rose-like flowers continually from June to first frost. They come in two sizes, the shorter ones ideal for ground cover and taller kinds for low hedges and mixed borders.

Among the good ground coverers, to 0.45m are *P. fruticosa* var. *arbuscula* with large yellow flowers: *P.f.* 'Abbotswood' AGM spreading branches to .75m with dark green leaves and many white flowers; *P.f.* 'Beesii' AGM, small yellow flowers and attractive silver green leaves; and *P.* 'Mandschurica' (syn. *P.f.* 'Manchu') white flowers on greyish foliage.

Potentilla fruticosa 'Red Ace'

Potentilla fruticosa 'Abbotswood'

Potentilla fruticosa 'Goldstar'

The taller cultivars come with a range of flower colours including: *P.f.* 'Goldfinger' AGM to 0.8m with large deep yellow flowers; *P.f.* 'Goldstar' very free flowering deep yellow over many weeks on a rather upright shrub to 0.8m; *P.f.* 'Katherine Dykes' AGM 1–2m, lemon yellow; *P.f.* 'Pretty Polly', 1m, neat pink; *P.f.* 'Primrose Beauty' AGM 0.8m; *P.f.* 'Princess' (syn. *P.f.* 'Blink') pale pink flowers fading to white, some flowers with extra petals to 0.6m in height and spreading to 1m; *P.f.* 'Red Ace' AGM to 0.75m, flame-red in cool weather conditions; and *P.f.* 'Tangerine' LA79 AGM, 1m with orange flowers which go yellow in hot sun.

Apart from their use in mixed shrubberies, as low hedges and for ground covering, cultivars of *Potentilla* are excellent for the back of rockeries, on sunny banks and in dry sunny sites close to walls.

Cultivation

All Potentillas are very easy to grow in any garden but the best results are obtained on lighter, well-drained soils.

The best flowering occurs on plants in full sun, although partial shade is tolerated. They need to be watered occasionally in dry weather and fed after the first main flush of flower to maintain a steady flow of new growth and flowers.

No regular pruning is necessary but vigour will be maintained if old and weak branches are cut back to ground level in spring. Regular light pruning of hedges is better than occasional hard cutting back, especially on older plants.

Propagate from cuttings taken with a heel in September/October rooted in frames.

Potentilla fruticosa 'Princess'

PRUNUS

Prunus laurocerasus – flower

Prunus laurocerasus – hedging

PRUNUS

Mention *Prunus* and most gardeners immediately think of the flamboyant flowering cherry trees rather than of *Prunus laurocerasus* AGM the "Common" or "Cherry Laurel" or a number of other useful hedge and shrub species within this large genera. Left unpruned *P. laurocerasus* forms a large spreading shrub to 5m, the rich shiny leaves being most attractive in the garden and when cut for large flower arrangements. It produces candles of small white flowers in April followed by red berries that turn black as they ripen.

Low-growing compact forms especially suited to ground cover 1m or so high are *P.l.* 'Otto Luyken' AGM and *P.l.* 'Zabeliana'. These grow quite well in problem areas such as under the shade of deciduous trees.

Cultivation

Virtually all garden soils are suitable for this easy-to-grow genera, an open sunny situation best suiting the deciduous kinds while the evergreens thrive in sun and shade.

P. tenella and *P. triloba* respond to quite hard pruning immediately after flowering. Strong new shoots are then produced, which flower the following spring.

Propagate the evergreens from cuttings made from side growths 25–30cm long in September and rooted in frames. These should be ready to plant out in six months.

The deciduous species are usually budded and grafted by nurserymen.

Gardeners can layer low branches in the autumn, roots usually having formed in 12 months, when the layer can be separated from the parent plant.

Prunus triloba

Prunus x cistena

Smaller in leaf size and with red leaf stalks, the "Portugal Laurel", *P. lusitanica* AGM is an even more elegant evergreen with hawthorn-scented white flowers which open in early summer. This is an easy-natured hardy plant growing in all soils, even in thin chalk.

There are several deciduous Prunus for hedges too, *Prunus x cistena*

Cultivation – Hedging

Plant the evergreens 70cm–1m apart and the deciduous types 0.35–0.5m, the closer planting for *P. x cistena*.

Newly-planted hedges are best pruned back by half in early spring after planting to make them branch freely from the base.

Evergreen hedges are best clipped in late summer with secateurs to avoid halving leaves.

AGM, commonly called "Crimson Dwarf" produces rich copper foliage after the blush-pink star-like flowers in April. An excellent plant for edging, to form low hedges to 1.5m, for formal beds and to use unclipped in mixed borders.

Much stronger-growing, up to 5m in height, is *Prunus cerasifera*, commonly called "Myrobalan" or "Cherry Plum" and its cultivars. The East Malling Rootstock for plum trees, Myrobalan 'B', is a clone also planted as hedging under the common name "Green Glow". Equally suitable for hedges are *P.c.* 'Pissardii' and *P.c.* 'Nigra' AGM, both having dark red young leaves that deepen almost to black with age and producing masses of pink buds opening white and blush-pink respectively.

There are also several ornamental flowering shrubs which make useful

garden plants. *Prunus tenella*, the "Dwarf Russian Almond" has thin, willow-like leaves on arching branches reaching 1m in height and spread. *P.t.* 'Fire Hill' AGM is a good cultivar with stems covered in rosy-crimson flowers ahead of the leaves in April.

A taller almond, often grown on a trunk to form a small standard tree to 2–3m is *Prunus triloba*. One of the earliest to flower, fully double pink flowers are produced along the length of the branches in March/April.

One other *Prunus* which must be mentioned even though it forms a very large shrub or smallish tree is *P. subhirtella* 'Autumnalis' AGM with clusters of small-semi-double white flowers from November to March. Planted towards the back of a large shrub border, it provides attractive autumn leaf colour, as do all these deciduous species.

PYRACANTHA

PYRACANTHA

The "Firethorns" have so many uses both in gardens and public landscaping that very extensive plantings have been and are being made. Modern cultivars provide sheets of white flowers in May and sumptuous clusters of berries year after year.

One of the very best is *Pyracantha* 'Orange Glow' AGM, a strong, fairly upright grower eventually to 4m with branches absolutely covered in orange-red fruits from October well into winter, if the birds leave them alone! P. 'Golden Charmer' is equally vigorous and with orange-yellow fruits. P. 'Mohave' has orange-red berries, which ripen early and hang on the plant for a long time. *P. coccinea* 'Red Column' makes a dense shrub with early-ripening scarlet berries and toothed glossy leaves.

P. rogersiana AGM has reddish-orange berries and *P.r.* 'Flava' AGM bright yellow berries; P. 'Saphyr Orange' is resistant to scab and useful for containers, while P. 'Saphyr Red" makes a good hedge and is resistant to scab and fireblight; P. 'Soleil d'Or' has golden-yellow berries; and P. 'Teton' has small orange-to-yellow berries and is one of the most resistant to fireblight.

Soft growth on young plants can be damaged by winter frost. Protecting new planting with fleece is advisable in cold weather.

Cultivation

All garden soils, including chalk, are suitable and the fire thorns thrive in both sun and partial shade and against walls, even those facing north and east. All new plants need to be container- or pot-grown because they do not take kindly to root disturbance and damage.

Most of them will grow to 4m as free-standing shrubs and up to 5m against walls. For hedges space them 0.6–1m apart.

They respond very well to pruning although it is difficult to decide when to prune. Do so in June after flowering and you remove developing berries, prune after the berries and you remove next year's flowers! Against walls, trim back after flowering and keep shortening new growth to form short flowering spurs. If you have the patience pruning every side shoot back to a bunch of set berries after petal fall will give a neat wall cover to 30cm deep.

May and June are the best months for any serious pruning, branches will shoot again well from quite hard cutting back. Propagation is by half-ripe cuttings in heated frames in July/August, it is easy to layer low branches in the autumn.

Scab disease causes black spots on the fruits and is controlled by systemic fungicide. Fireblight can be a problem and in areas where this disease is common resistant cultivars should be tried.

Tip

The fierce thorns of *Pyracantha* help to create impenetrable barriers and they are marvellous plants to deter vandals. Plant one side of a wall and no one will climb over it.

Pyracantha 'Orange Glow'

Pyracantha coccinea 'Red Column'

Pyracantha 'Golden Charmer'

Pyracantha 'Soleil d'Or'

Pyracantha 'Mohave'

RHODODENDRON

RHODODENDRON

Extensive woodland with broad walks lined with noble trees is perhaps the perfect setting for banks of the stately large-flowered *Rhododendron* cultivars. They can also play a colourful part in gardens of modest size. Some, like *Rhododendron* 'Pink Pearl', may in time outgrow a limited space and become bare at the base. They can be rejuvenated and reduced in size by cutting the branches hard back in April.

Most garden centres offer a range of cultivars in three size groups. Good examples in the larger shrub size, growing to over 2m in time, are *R.* 'Gomer Waterer' AGM, white flushed pale lilac; *R.* 'Hotei' AGM, deep yellow (keep out of full sun); *R.* 'Purple Splendour' AGM; *R.* 'Sappho' AGM, white with deep purple throat; and *R.* 'Wilgen's Ruby' AGM, deep

Rhododendrons in containers

All rhododendrons demand acid soils and where the ideal conditions do not occur naturally it is worth creating them artificially or growing the more dwarf types in pots.

A well-drained, lime-free sandy loam enriched with such organic matter as well-rotted leaves (ideally a mix of pine and oak), bracken, rotted cow manure and/or peat suits them best. Plants in containers need an ericaceous compost, that is an acidic one.

red. *R.* 'President Roosevelt' has good leaf variegation as well as ice-pink, red-edged flowers.

Among the semi-dwarf May-flowering ones, cultivars of *R. yakushimanum* reign supreme, *R.y.* 'Koichiro Wada' AGM is deep pink in bud opening to almost white and forming a neat rounded bush to 1.2m with silvery-green young leaves maturing to shiny-green above and felty-brown beneath. Good hybrids include *R.* 'Doc' AGM, light pink and very hardy; *R.* 'Golden Torch' AGM, salmon-pink buds opening pale yellow; *R.* 'Percy Wiseman', compact, pink; and *R.* 'Titian Beauty' AGM, geranium-red flowers May and June.

Many blue and lavender flowers

Rhododendrons in parkland setting

Tip

Leaves which quickly turn pale green and then yellow will have come into contact with traces of lime and chalk. This chlorosis can be overcome by repeated watering with iron sequestrene, usually present in acidic fertilisers. Heavy applications of flowers of sulphur at 100–150gm per square metre and/or heavy enrichment with peat will reduce alkalinity.

An alternative to container planting is the construction of beds, above the water drainage level and filled with peaty soil.

Cultivation

Rhododendrons need to be grown in an acidic soil, free from lime. See the information and tip boxes about growing rhododendrons in containers or raised beds as alternative planting possibilities where unsuitable soil conditions prevail.

Be sure these plants do not lack moisture, leaf edges curling down and leaf tips going black is a sure sign of drought. For this reason, semi-shaded sites suit most kinds and regular mulching to keep roots moist is needed in sunny positions. Rhododendrons benefit from an acidic-high nitrogen fertiliser in spring. Avoid feeding after late June to prevent getting leafy growth at the expense of flower.

Their surface fibrous roots do allow for easy transplanting of even large plants in full flower. Just dig out with as much root as possible and keep well watered until re-established.

The only annual pruning is the removal of dead flowers, best done by snapping out with finger and thumb. Hard pruning to rejuvenate leggy branches can be done immediately after flowering.

Propagation for gardeners is by layering.

Vine weevil is a real pest, the adults bite notches out of the leaves in summer and autumn, a sure sign they are present. Their larvae do the real damage by chewing off roots. Biological controls or spraying and soil insecticides are necessary to control them.

The disease Rhododendron bud Blast, which causes flower buds to turn grey and brown in winter and develop black bristle-like growths in spring, is carried by a leaf hopper. Control this pest with malathion or some similar insecticide in August/September.

are found among the dwarf April-flowering types, which generally do better in full sun and include: *R.* 'Blue Diamond', rich lavender-blue; *R.* 'Blue Tit', lavender-blue deepening with age; *R. impeditum* AGM, purplish-blue; and *R.* 'Praecox' AGM, lilac-pink early March. All these may need light cover to protect the flowers on frosty nights in spring. Other flower colours are provided by such hybrids as *R.* 'Curlew' AGM, bright yellow in May'; *R.* 'Patty Bee' AGM, pale yellow with dark green leaves which bronze in winter; and *R.* 'Scarlet Wonder' AGM, mid April.

Plants with pale green leaves should be watered with sequestred iron in spring to green them up.

Rhododendron 'Curlew'

Rhododendron 'Purple Splendour'

Rhododendron 'Percy Wiseman'

RHUS

RHUS

The "Sumachs", *Rhus glabra* and *Rhus typhina*, are too often dismissed because of their ease of culture and good nature. They are especially eye-catching when the leaf colour changes in the autumn.

R. glabra, the "Smooth Sumach" is the smaller in size, growing 3m high and 2m across and, as the common name suggests, has no hairs on the young shoots. Female plants produce conical light red flower clusters 12cm high in July, followed by dark red seed pods.

"Stag's Horn Sumach", *R. typhina* is larger, growing to 5m in height and spread and is by far the most commonly found in gardens. Densely-packed cone-shaped flowers 15cm long are produced in June/July on the female plants, followed again by crimson seed heads. Male plants have

Cultivation

Any ordinary garden soil is suitable for *Rhus*, a sunny site producing the best autumn leaf colour. They withstand city grime and are suitable for use as individual specimen plants and in mixed shrub borders.

Pruning is not required although if these plants, once established, are cut really hard back in February/March each year they produce vigorous shoots with luxuriant leaves 36cm long.

Rhus have a tendency to sucker around the base, these suckers being somewhat invasive and a nuisance in small gardens.

Propagation is by half-ripe cuttings in summer rooted in a frame and, more easily, by lifting suckers from October onwards.

a smaller, green flower spike. Both have cultivars called 'Laciniata' which have deeply-cut fern-like leaves. Plants of both sexes are needed to set seeds.

Rhus typhina 'Laciniata'

Rhus typhina

Ribes sanguineum

RIBES

Some of the shrubs most commonly found in gardens in spring are the "Flowering Currants", the best known species of which is *Ribes sanguineum* growing to 3m high, 2m across and flowering in April.

Good cultivars include: *R.s.* 'Brocklebankii' AGM, slow-growing, yellow leaved with pink flowers; *R.s.* 'King Edward VII', a little smaller than the species with crimson flowers; *R.s.* 'Pulborough Scarlet' AGM of upright habit good for hedges and with deep red flowers; *R. s.* 'Tydeman's White' AGM (syn. R. Roseum 'Tydeman's White') is a good white-flowered form.

The "Buffalo Currant", *Ribes odoratum* has shiny green leaves that turn mid yellow in autumn, the April flowers being yellow and nicely clove-scented.

Cultivation

Ribes are not demanding shrubs, growing well in all soils and situations including full sun and partial shade. Flowering will be improved and more brightly coloured in full sun.

Pruning consists of the removal of a few older branches immediately after flowering. Alternatively prune out some well-budded shoots in early spring and force into early flower indoors in water. Give these plants some growmore fertiliser after pruning to encourage strong new replacement shoots.

Propagation is very easy from hardwood cuttings 30–37cm long inserted into sandy soil in October/November.

ROMNEYA

The "Tree Poppy" or "California Poppy", *Romneya coulteri* AGM is something of a mixture between herbaceous perennial and shrub.

Stunning, poppy-like single blooms 12cm across are produced from July to October.

Romneya coulteri

Cultivation

Romneya requires a sheltered sunny site and is not hardy in the colder areas of Britain. In a light, well-drained soil, stems will reach up to 2m high and the suckering habit will allow the plant to slowly spread.

Young plants are best cut down in October and covered with bracken or straw for winter protection.

Propagation is by root cuttings in frames in February. These plants do not take kindly to root disturbance, however, and it might be better to transplant suckers which grow some distance from the main plant in April.

Ribes odoratum

Ribes sanguineum

Rosa moyesii 'Geranium'

ROSA

There are very many excellent complete books on roses, here I can do no more than whet your appetite for the many quite delightful shrub roses. Left to grow with naturally arching branches, like the wild "Dog Rose" under gentle restraint, they are a real joy in many garden situations.

We are spoilt for choice, from species and old cultivars to the latest introduction. The "Cabbage Rose", *Rosa* x *centifolia*, includes *R.* x *c.* 'Cristata' AGM, the "Crested Moss Rose" and *R.* x *c.* 'Muscosa; AGM, the 'Moss Rose' popular with gardeners and painters since the 18th century.

The richly-scented "Damask Rose", *R.* x *damascena* thought to have been brought to Europe by the crusaders in the 16th century, is used to make the fragrant oil Attar of Roses. *R.* x *d. versicolor* (the York and Lancaster roses) has double flowers, some white, some pink and white and some pink.

Rosa moyesii

Early-flowering yellow shrub roses are well represented by *R.* x 'Catabrigiensis' AGM with fern-like leaves and *R. xanthina* 'Canary Bird' AGM which makes an excellent weeping standard. Most spectacular in flower are such cultivars as *R.* 'Fruhlingsgold' AGM, fragrant, light yellow and *R.* 'Nevada' AGM, creamy-white.

For flowers and brightly coloured fruits choose the taller-growing, to 2m *R. moyesii* a dark red single, its more compact hybrid *R.m.* 'Geranium' with larger fruits, *R. glauca* (syn. *R. rubrifolia*) AGM with rich purple leaves and stems and deep pink flowers followed by dark red hips and, for ground covering, *R. rugosa* 'Frau Dagmar Hastrop' with rich crinkled green leaves and rose-pink flowers followed by round, plump crimson hips.

Cultivation

Rosa all grow easily and need no more than the occasional old stems removed after flowering. *Rosa glauca* gives the best leaf colour if pruned hard in spring but this means fewer flowers and hips.

Commercially they are propagated by budding onto special rootstocks in summer. Gardeners can root hardwood cuttings outside in sandy soil in early autumn fairly easily.

Rosa 'Fruhlingsgold'

Rosa rugosa 'Frau Dagmar Hastrop'

ROSMARINUS

The very popular aromatic shrub "Rosemary" makes a good partner to "Old English Lavender", both revelling in warm, sunny sites. *Rosmarinus officinalis*, with grey-green leaves and blue flowers in late spring, has been grown in Britain for over 400 years. There are a number of good garden cultivars including: *R.o.* 'Miss Jessopp's Upright' AGM is useful for short-term low hedges; *R.o.* 'Sissinghurst Blue' AGM is a compact form with blue flowers; and *R.o.* 'Severn Sea' AGM is a dwarf plant with bright blue flowers.

Rosemary is attractive in the front of shrub borders, a good plant to grow in patio pots as well as, of course, for flavouring food.

Cultivation

All free-draining soils are suitable – these plants are short-lived in heavy, wet situations, especially when winters are cold.

Half-ripe cuttings root easily in July/August. Prune after flowering.

RUBUS

There are quite a lot of ornamental brambles grown for flower and stem colour, some rather invasive. *Rubus* 'Benenden' AGM is a lovely thornless deciduous shrub to 3m with single

Rubus thibetanus

white flowers, *R. cockburnianus* AGM has bright white arching stems to 2m and R.c. 'Golden Vale' is equally eye-catching but with yellow leaves. *R. thibetanus* 'Siver Fern' AGM is another blue-white barked cultivar with fern-like leaves.

Cultivation

Most garden soils are suitable for *Rubus*. Ornamental-stemmed varieties should have the old stems cut out after flowering.

Propagate spreading types by division from October to March, others by half-ripe cuttings in summer.

RUTA

Commonly called "Rue", *Ruta graveolens* 'Jackman's Blue" AGM is a compact deciduous shrub to 1m. This popular herb can cause a skin rash, especially when handled in strong sunlight.

Ruta graveolens 'Jackman's Blue'

Cultivation

Ruta grows well in sunny, free-draining soil.

Plants can be trimmed back to old wood in April and propagation is by cuttings taken in August and rooted in frames.

Rosmarinus officinalis

RUSCUS

RUSCUS

"Butcher's Broom" is a curious evergreen sub-shrub, there being male and female plants of *Ruscus aculeatus*, the female producing bright red berries in the autumn.

Cultivation

Ruscus survive in most soils and situations, including dry shade under trees.

What appear to be leaves are in fact flattened stems and cut branches have become popular to use in flower arrangements.

Propagation is by division of the suckering shoots.

SALIX

The different kinds of willow number in hundreds, many growing to tree proportions. Several quite strong growers are kept down in size by pruning hard each spring to

Ruscus aculeatus

encourage new shoots, which have brightly-coloured bark.

Good examples are *Salix alba vitellina* 'Britzensis' AGM, the "Scarlet Willow", *S.a. vitellina* AGM (syn. S.a. 'Chermesina'), the "Golden Willow"

Cultivation

Any ordinary garden soil is suitable for willows, especially those on the damp side. Here is a group of shrubs that withstand waterlogging. Light, dry soils will need the addition of well-rotted compost to retain moisture if strong growth with good coloured bark is to be achieved.

Little pruning, if any, is needed for the more dwarf kinds apart from the removal of dead wood. Allow the coloured-barked species to get established before pruning hard back every other spring in average soils and every spring in moist, fertile soils.

Propagation is by hardwood cuttings.

and *S. x rubens* 'Basfordiana' AGM which has bright orange-red bark.

Large garden owners who like willow stems for cutting to arrange in water should consider *S. x stipularis* (syn. *S. x smithiana*) with silver-grey catkins in spring and *S. caprea*, the "Goat Willow" or "Pussy Willow". For Japanese arrangements gardeners

Salix integra 'Hakuro-nishiki

Salix helvetica

Salix caprea 'Kilmarnock'

plant with the species producing typical bluish-purple salvia-shaped flowers in June/July. There is an attractive non-flowering form which makes good short term ground cover.

S.o. 'Icterina' AGM has green and gold leaves as well as a low, spreading habit. S.o. 'Purpurascens' AGM, the "Purple-leaved Sage" looks very good to the front of shrub borders and in patio pots and S.o. 'Tricolor' is the least hardy, having grey-green leaves edged white to cream, the young shoots overlaid pink.

Cultivation

All *Salvia* are relatively short-lived and do best in full sun. They need a light, free-draining soil and given this survive quite severe winter frost. Young plants make good autumn foliage plants for patio pots. Propagation is by rooting softwood cuttings in summer.

Young plants respond well to shearing back in spring but old woody plants may not grow away very well after hard pruning.

Salvia officinalis 'Purpurascens'

should try S. *udensis* 'Sekka' for its curiously twisted and contorted stems.

More in keeping with other shrubs in this book and of more modest size are: S.c. 'Kilmarnock' AGM grafted on a 1.6m stem to form a small weeping tree, S. *lanata* AGM the silver-green-leaved "Woolly Willow", slow-growing to 1m, S. *hastata* 'Wehrhahnii' AGM the naked branches of which carry slender silver catkins which stand like stalagmites and S. *helvetica* AGM, a pretty, compact shrub with silver-grey catkins and grey-green leaves in spring.

The very pretty white-tinged-pink-leaved S. *integra* 'Hakuro-nishiki' is lovely in new leaf but can scorch in hot sun. There are even ground coverers like S. *repens argentea* AGM with creeping stems covered with silver-green leaves and yellow catkins in spring.

SALVIA

The evergreen sages are both ornamental in the coloured-leaved forms and very popular culinary herbs. *Salvia officinalis*, the "Common Sage" is a dwarf, almost evergreen shrubby

SAMBUCUS

Sambucus nigra 'Guincho Purple'

Cultivation

All garden soils are suitable for this hardy deciduous shrub.

Those plants of *Sambucus* grown for their coloured leaves can be pruned back hard in early spring to stimulate strong new shoots. This restricts their size. Alternatively cut back one third of the branches each spring to keep regenerating the growth.

Propagation is by hardwood cuttings in winter and also by half-ripe cuttings in summer.

Sambucus racemosa 'Plumosa Aurea'

SAMBUCUS

The "Common Elderberry", *Sambucus nigra* is something of a weed tree, its flat white flower heads are used for cordials and the black fruits for wine and flavouring apple pies. There are several good garden forms such as: *S.n.* 'Aurea' AGM with golden-yellow leaves; *S.n.* 'Guincho Purple' AGM (syn. *S.n.* 'Purpurea') with purple leaves; and *S. racemosa* 'Plumosa Aurea' with finely-cut golden-yellow leaves.

Flowers of all kinds have a rather insipid scent; some of the yellow-leaved forms can scorch in full sun. The cut-leaved forms are slightly less vigorous, to 2m in height and spread.

SANTOLINA

This aromatic silver-leaved low shrub is commonly called "Cotton Lavender". Santolinas are widely used to the front of shrub borders, among perennial flowers and as low hedging in knot gardens. Rather like lavender young plants respond well to regular clipping and are good subjects for patio pots and window boxes.

The most common species is *Santolina chamaecyparissus* AGM with yellow button-type flowers in summer and good silver foliage to 70cm high. *S.c.* 'Lambrook Silver' forms a low mound of feathery silver leaves, while *S.c.* 'Pretty Carol' is even more compact, to 30cm.

Santolina chamaecyparissus

Cultivation

All soils are suitable for *Santolina* as long as they are well-drained and in a light position, if not in the ideal, full sun.

Trim over lightly in spring to retain plant shape but avoid cutting into old wood on old plants.

Half-ripe cuttings root easily in summer.

Sarcococca hookeriana var. digyna

SARCOCOCCA

A very short evergreen shrub, *Sarcococca hookeriana* var. *digyna* AGM, the "Christmas Box", grows eventually to 1m. It has very fragrant small white male flowers in late winter and the smaller female flowers on the same stems produce black berries. *S. ruscifolia chinensis* AGM has dark red berries.

Cultivation

Sarcococca grow in all soils, including chalk, and withstand dense shade.

They require no pruning and are propagated by digging up some of the suckers in early autumn: a great plant to bring fragrance to patio pots in winter.

SENECIO (syn. Brachyglottis)

A plant popular for its felty-silver leaves, *Senecio greyii* and its better form *S.* 'Sunshine' AGM with greyish silver-leaves grow to about 1m in height and spread. Excellent seaside plants, producing yellow daisy-style flowers in summer.

It is a matter of personal choice whether these yellow flowers are left in place, some people feel the colour clashes with the silver leaves.

Cultivation

All shrubby senecios grow in a wide range of soil types but need full sun and free-draining conditions in winter.

They can be pruned back in spring to rejuvenate older plants which may be bare at the base.

Propagation is by half-ripe cuttings, in frames, in summer.

Senecio greyii

SKIMMIA

SKIMMIA

The dramatic increase in patio pot gardening has made *Skimmia* very popular because they provide evergreen foliage and eye-catching winter flower bud colour. They make neat, dwarf shrubs growing eventually to 1m in height and spread.

All but one are single-sexed, both male and female plants being needed to set berries on the females at the ratio one male to three females. The male plants do, however, flower the more freely: the brilliant red berries remain on the female bushes for up to twelve months.

Skimmia x *confusa* 'Kew Green' AGM is a male with large heads of off-white fragrant flowers. Most

Skimmia japonica 'Rubella'

commonly offered are cultivars of *S. japonica*, with *S.j.* ssp. *reevesiana* the hermaphrodite form with self-pollinating flowers. A single plant of *S.j.* ssp. *r.* 'Robert Fortune' AGM will provide fragrant flowers and berries but, unlike other *S. japonica* cultivars, does not grow well in chalky soils.

S.j. 'Fragrans' AGM is male, very free-flowering and fragrant; *S.j.* 'Nymans' AGM is female, very free-fruiting when pollinated and has large fruits; *S.j.* 'Rubella' AGM is male and the best for its bright red buds right through the winter and fragrant white spring flowers.

Tip

Thousands of plants of S.j. 'Rubella' are grown annually for winter window box use. Often they are grown in rock-wool and similar chunky free-draining material.

While they are cheaply priced such plants do not transplant well into gardens. Grow them for a year or so first in ericaceous compost to develop a tougher root system.

Skimmia japonica

Cultivation

While most skimmias grow well in both slightly acid and slightly alkaline soils, they do need partial shade and a free-draining soil enriched with plenty of organic matter to retain moisture in summer.

Grown in full sun and allowed to dry out in summer, the leaves blanch and become very small.

They do not need pruning although old plants can be regenerated by pruning back some old branches in spring.

Propagate by half-ripe cuttings in summer and hardwood cuttings in late autumn, both in cold frames.

SOLANUM

A useful group of free-flowering semi-evergreen climbing plants of the potato family and with potato-like flowers.

Solanum crispum 'Glasnevin' AGM will grow to 6m scrambling over a fence or trellis, with purple flowers from midsummer to the frost.

For white flowers choose *S. jasminoides* 'Album' AGM which grows even stronger to 9m but requires more protection in the form of a south-facing wall in all but the warmest gardens.

Cultivation

All soils are suitable for *Solanum* if in full sun. Some protection may be needed for both species in hard winters.

To prune just thin out excessive growth and remove frost-damaged stems in spring.

Softwood cuttings root easily in summer.

Spartium junceum

Solanum jasminoides 'Album'

SPARTIUM

The "Spanish Broom", *Spartium junceum* AGM is a close relative of *Cytisus*, with rush-like stems and bright yellow, fragrant pea-shaped flowers in May/June and through the summer.

Of rather loose habit, it will reach 3m in a few years.

Cultivation

Spartium grow in all well-drained soils, including those by the sea, and a sunny position are the ideal. Leggy plants can be sheared back in spring but, like the "Brooms", not into old wood.

They are easily raised from seed and self-sown seedlings can often be found in gardens.

Again like brooms, they are best raised in pots because they do not take kindly to root damage when transplanting.

SPIRAEA

Spiraea x arguta

Spiraea japonica 'Goldflame'

SPIRAEA

This very useful group of garden shrubs is best considered in two groups, the taller spring-flowering Spiraeas with mostly white blooms and the shorter summer-flowering species with pink to carmine flowers, many of these plants having coloured foliage on the young shoots.

Most prolific flowering are: *Spiraea* x *arguta* to 1.5m with large maidenhair fern-like foliage of lovely light green, suited to infilling in flower arrangements and masses of white bloom on arching branches; *S.* x *cinerea* 'Grefsheim' AGM is also compact; *S. thunbergii* AGM is a little coarser to 2m and one of the first to flower; *S.* x *vanhouttei* AGM is even more vigorous, to 2.5m; and *S.* x *v.* 'Pink Ice' has pink-coloured branch tips with leaves opening a mottled white and green. *S. nipponica* 'Snowmound' AGM forms a mound of stems 1–1.5m covered in white flowers in early summer.

The summer-flowering species usually have pink or carmine-red flowers in clusters or spikes and include: *Spiraea japonica* 'Anthony Waterer' AGM, flat heads of deep carmine-red flowers from midsummer, the new shoots often variegated cream and pink; *S.j.* 'Candle Light' has gold-to-bronze new shoots in spring; *S.j.* 'Fire Light' bronze-to-yellow leaves; *S.j.* 'Goldflame' AGM has rich copper new shoots turning soft yellow then light red; and *S.j.* 'Magic Carpet' has very rich copper

Cultivation

All these hardy shrubs are easy to grow, undemanding in respect of soil type and situation and well worth wide garden use. Spiraeas are best in full sun to partial shade and in soils with some moisture in summer.

Most of the pink summer-flowering kinds with colourful young shoots need hard pruning in early spring each year once well established. It can be worth cutting half of the stems hard and lightly tipping the rest: the lightly-tipped branches then provide very early spring colour and the hard-pruned ones produce strong new shoots a littler later.

White spring flowering kinds need no more than a few of the older stems pruned out after flowering.

Propagation is by hardwood cuttings in late autumn and by half ripe cuttings in frames in summer.

young growth, quite good summer leaf colour and good autumn colour. All these grow to 0.75m or thereabouts and are used more for foliage colour than flower.

Quite unusual is *S. japonica* 'Shirobana' AGM with white and pink flower heads on the same stem from July to September. *S. x billiardii* 'Triumphans' grows to 1.5m and produces long spikes of deep pink flowers in summer.

STACHYURUS

A useful early-flowering shrub, *Stachyurus praecox* AGM has long tassles of pale yellow flowers late winter and early spring.

Cultivation
Stachyurus grows well in most soils and sun or some shade.

Little pruning is needed save the removal of a few old stems occasionally from the base.

Propagate from cuttings taken with a heel in July and rooted in heated frames.

STRANVAESIA syn. *Photinia*
An excellent large shrub for autumn leaf colour, *Stranvaesia davidiana* syn. *Photinia davidiana* has upright growth and narrow evergreen leaves, the oldest of which turn bright red in the autumn. Hawthorn-like flowers on *Stranvaesia* set to produce bright red fruits in the autumn.

Stachyurus praecox

Stranvaesia davidiana

Cultivation
All reasonable garden soils are suitable for *Stranvaesia* including some chalk.

Propagate by half-ripe cuttings in summer in frames.

No pruning is required.

Spiraea japonica 'Anthony Waterer'

Spiraea japonica 'Shirobana'

SYMPHORICARPOS

SYMPHORICARPOS

The "Snowberry", *Symphoricarpos*, is a suckering, deciduous shrub to 1.5m high with slender stems and tiny blush-white flowers between June and August. These are followed by bright white berries which hang on for many months if left unattacked by birds.

Commonly found in Britain is *Symphoricarpos albus* which grows to 2m high and carries white fruits. Better garden shrubs are provided by the cultivars: *S. x doorenbosii* 'Magic Berry' with rose-pink fruits; *S. x d.* 'Mother of Pearl', white fruits tinged pink; and *S. x d.* 'White Hedge', with erect and compact growth forming a natural hedge with clusters of small white berries.

There are variegated leaf forms such as: *S. orbiculatus* 'Foliis Variegatis' with oval leaves edged yellow. One of the best for ground cover is *S. x chenaultii* 'Hancock' with wide-spreading low dense habit and pinkish fruits.

Cultivation

All soils are suitable for *Symphoricarpos* and they spread easily even under the dense shade of trees: can be used in shrub borders, to furnish wilder parts of the gardens and to quickly fill watersides and banks.

Propagation is by lifting suckers in the dormant season or taking hardwood cuttings in winter. The only pruning needed is the complete removal of a few old branches in early spring.

SYRINGA

There are few shrubs better than the *Syringa vulgaris* cultivars for cutting, fragrance and garden decoration. This is among the most popular of garden plants, growing ultimately 4–5m high and blooming from late April to early June. The terminal buds on each branch develop into flower clusters in pairs or even fours in colours ranging from pure white, primrose and pink to purple, red, mauve, violet and lilac-blue.

Most nurseries and garden centres offer both single and double forms: the following are good examples. *S.v.* 'Charles Joly' AGM, deep purple-red double; *S.v.* 'Edward J. Gardner', pale pink double; *S.v.* 'Souvenir de Louis Spaeth' AGM (syn. *S.v.* 'Andenken

Symphoricarpos albus

Syringa vulgaris

Syringa x persica

Syringa microphylla 'Superba'

an Ludwig Späth' AGM), deep purple single, one of the best, free flowering; *S.v.* 'Katherine Havemeyer' AGM, double purple; *S.v.* 'Michel Buchner', double lilac; and *S.v.* 'Mrs Edward Harding' AGM, claret-red double.

Extend the season of flowers with some of the species, several of which make much smaller shrubs: S. x *josiflexa* 'Bellicent' AGM has enormous panicles of rose pink flowers that weep down in May; S. meyeri 'Palibin' AGM to 1.8m is slow-growing and has violet-purple flowers in May and sometimes again in September; S. x *persica*, lilac May flowers and S. *microphylla* 'Superba' AGM, to 1.5m rose-pink flowers from May to September.

The so-called "Canadian Hybrids", S. x *prestoniae*, are very hardy and later flowering, into early summer: a good example is S. x *p*. 'Elinor' AGM fairly erect with pale lavender flower heads.

Cultivation

Syringa thrive in most well cultivated garden soils including chalk. Hungry plants, their masses of fibrous roots quickly impoverish poor soils.

The best flowers occur in full sun, the flowers on shaded plants tending to be thin and less impressive.

Cutting branches while they are in flower for indoor decoration is a good way of pruning.

Occasional hard pruning after flowering does give strong new growth and bigger trusses of flower.

Named cultivars are propagated by grafting, not a job for the average gardener. A watch should be kept for suckers from grafted plants: these are likely to produce few, very thin, poor flowers.

TAMARIX

The "Tamarisks" form quite large deciduous shrubs with fine green leaves and masses of tiny pink flowers clustered in short spikes, which cascade from arching branches.

Quite strong-growing to 4m is *Tamarix tentrandra* AGM flowering in May ahead of the leaves on the previous year's wood.

Later flowering in July and August and brighter pink is *T. ramosissima* (syn. *T. pentandra*) and its even darker form *T.r.* 'Rubra' AGM growing little over 3m even in ideal conditions. These two flower on the current year's growth.

They all have a graceful habit which makes them attractive in mixed

Cultivation

Despite the light, delicate appearance tamarisks are tough in constitution and easy to grow in most garden soils. Well-drained and sunny sites and even quite poor soils will give good growth.

The early-flowering species should be cut back after flowering, the later ones in winter or early spring.

Propagation is by hardwood cuttings taken in October and rooted easily in open, sandy soil.

borders, standing alone, in informal hedges, beside walls and by the waterside. Tolerant of wind and sea spray, they are useful coastal plants.

TEUCRIUM

Members of the sage family, the "Shrubby Germander", *Teucrium fruticans* has evergreen leaves dense white and felty in appearance on the undersides, pale blue flowers in summer. *T.f.* 'Azureum' AGM has darker-blue flowers and is slightly more tender.

Cultivation

Teucrium require a well-drained soil, sunny site and protection in all but the warmest gardens. Pruning is best done in spring by lightly clipping back, up to one half, last summer's growth. Propagate by half-ripe cuttings in summer in frames.

Tamarix tentrandra

Teucrium fruticans

Vaccinium corymbosum

VACCINIUM

Grown for their autumn colour and fruits, the "Highbush Blueberry", *Vaccinium corymbosum* AGM is an excellent dual purpose plant. They grow very well in tubs of ericaceous compost to provide jade green flowers in May, light green leaves all summer, delicious purple fruits and yellow-to-scarlet purple leaves in autumn before the fall.

There are many named cultivars and cropping will be heaviest where there are two different ones for cross pollination.

Choose *V. vitis-idaea* 'Koralle' AGM for dwarf creeping ground cover. A type of "Cowberry" with neat round evergreen leaves, white bell-shaped flowers tinged pink and

Tip
Blueberries make excellent container plants when grown in ericaceous compost. Watered well and fed occasionally a four-year plant will produce pounds of fruit.

bright red berries.

The "Cranberry" is another compact, dense evergreen shrub with red flowers and purplish-black berries. It is correctly called *V. macrocarpon*: there are several named cultivars, such as *V.m.* 'Hamilton".

Cultivation
Vaccinium do need acid soil and naturally grow in damp acid heathland. When planting in mixed borders enrich the soil with peat and feed with acidic fertilisers in spring.

Propagation is by half-ripe cuttings in summer and hardwood cuttings in late autumn, both in frames. Pruning is no more than the removal of some old stems each spring.

VIBURNUM

There is such variety in the 70-plus different species of *Viburnum* that one could almost have a garden furnished with them alone. Broadly divided into deciduous and evergreen types, they have either white or white flushed pink flowers. Several have a lovely fragrance and others carry richly-coloured fruits and brightly-coloured leaves in the autumn.

The deciduous kinds can be divided again into summer- and winter-to-early-spring flowering. First to flower is *Viburnum farreri* AGM (syn. *V. fragrans*) with small clusters of pink buds and fragrant white flowers on the bare branches from November to March. It grows fairly upright, to 4m in height and 3m spread, and the young leaves are rich bronze in colour.

Viburnum x bodnantense 'Dawn'

VIBURNUM

Viburnum plicatum 'Mariesii'

Viburnum opulus 'Roseum'

V. x *b.* 'Anne Russell' AGM is more compact but less evergreen and *V.b.* 'Park Farm Hybrid' AGM has larger flower clusters from mid to late spring.

Our native species *V. opulus,* commonly called "Guelder Rose", can be seen in hedgerows especially when the translucent scarlet berries colour in late summer.

The "Snowball Tree", *Viburnum opulus* 'Roseum' AGM (syn. *V.o.* 'Sterile') is a well-known and an appropriately common-named summer flowering shrub. It can be forced into flower early, the opening flowers being tinted green.

Free-fruiting cultivars include: *V.o.* 'Compactum' AGM which can scorch in sun; *V.o.* 'Notcutt's Variety' AGM, a strong-growing plant with larger flowers and fruits; and *V.o.* 'Xanthocarpum' AGM with clear yellow fruits. Even more showy in flower than the "Snowball Trees" are *V. plicatum* 'Lanarth', quite vigorous-growing and fairly upright and *V.p.* 'Mariesii' AGM with tiered branches and good autumn leaf colour. Extra colour is provided by *V.p.* 'Pink Beauty' AGM whose white flowers age into shades of pink.

The evergreen types are of equal value in the garden. Winter-flowering *Viburnum tinus,* commonly called "Laurustinus" can be used as an excellent replacement for laurel. Apart from the pink buds and white flower trusses produced through autumn and winter it forms an excellent hedge and informal screen, withstanding shade, seaside conditions, wind and a very wide range of

More flowers and a stronger rose-pink colouring is provided by two clones of the hybrid *V.* x *bodnantense* which has *V. farreri* as a parent. Both *V.* x *b.* 'Dawn' AGM with rose-pink flowers and *V.* x *b.* 'Deben' AGM with flowers opening white have blooms which survive quite hard frost.

Flowering in April and May but with larger heads of flower is *V. carlesii* one of the most sweetly scented of all shrubs and a very popular garden plant. Slow-growing, it eventually reaches 2m high and 1.5m spread.

There are two more compact hybrids with even larger flower clusters, up to 11cm across, *V.* x *carlcephalum* AGM with richly-coloured autumn leaves and *V.* x *juddii* AGM which is said to be more aphid resistant. *V.* x *burkwoodii* has *V. carlesii* as a parent but is evergreen and flowers from late winter into spring.

Tip

Viburnum make good container plants and scent a conservatory if brought in, in bud to flower under glass.

Vibrunum carlesii

All *Viburnum* grow and flourish in a wide range of soil types. Well-cultivated soils with sufficient organic matter to retain moisture are the ideal. Some species really thrive in chalk, for example *V. rhytidophyllum* which can be used in such soils to provide the shape and form of rhododendrons.

Pruning is not required except perhaps to thin out old and damaged wood after flowering.

Propagation is for the most part by half-ripe cuttings of the evergreens and softwood cuttings of deciduous kinds, in frames in summer. The scented spring-flowering kinds are grafted, not a job for home gardeners.

Aphids can be a problem on several of the deciduous Viburnum: suitable sprays should be applied on first sightings of their presence.

soil types. It grows to 3m in height and spread – for smaller sizes choose *V.t.* 'Eve Price' AGM with flowers tinged pink and *V.t.* 'Gwenllian' AGM, both having smaller leaves than the species and setting deep blue-black fruits.

Finally and mainly for foliage effect there are: the low-growing, ground-covering *V. davidii* AGM which has inconspicuous whitish flowers in June followed by turquoise-blue berries; and the much taller *V. rhytidophyllum* growing to over 3m with large white flower-heads in May/June and red fruits which turn black in the autumn. Both require planting in groups to ensure pollination and the production of berries.

Viburnum tinus 'Eve Price'

Vibrunum rhytidophyllum

Viburnum davidii

WEIGELA

WEIGELA

The free-flowering and easy to grow nature of *Weigela* has made it one of the most popular deciduous garden shrubs. *Weigela florida* grows to 2m in height and spread with trumpet-shaped flowers red in bud opening rose pink in late spring and early summer. *W.f.* 'Foliis Purpureis' AGM is a little more compact, having dark purplish-green leaves and deep pink flowers; *W.f.* 'Variegata' is an excellent green-and-cream-variegated-leaved cultivar with good autumn colour and pale pink flowers.

There is quite a range of hybrids, including: *W.* 'Abel Carrière' AGM with rose-pink flowers; *W.* 'Bristol Ruby' with dark red flowers in May/June and often a small second flush in the autumn; *W.* 'Briant Rubidor' has carmine flowers and pale yellow leaves which can scorch in hot sun; *W.* 'Eva Rathke' a good red with upright growth to 1.5m, and *W.* 'Mont Blanc' AGM is a good white.

Cultivation

Weigela thrive in well-cultivated garden soils, preferably not too light and sandy, where they give vigorous growth: both full sun and partial shade are acceptable.

They look well in mixed borders, against fences and to provide a low screen. Planted with *Pyracantha* behind and adjacent to purple-leaved *Berberis*, the variegated form looks stunning from September to November.

Pruning quite hard immediately after flowering gives strong new growth and the best ornamental effect.

Easy to propagate from hardwood and softwood cuttings.

Weigela 'Eva Rathke'

Weigela florida 'Variegata'

WISTERIA

The two most popular species are *Wisteria floribunda*, the "Japanese Wisteria" with 13–19 leaflets per leaf and clockwise-twining stems and *W. sinensis* AGM, the "Chinese Wisteria', most leaves of which have 9–13 leaflets and which has anticlockwise-twining stems. Both are superb plants once well established and an absolute joy in May when the great trusses of fragrant mauve flowers 20cm and more in length hang from leafless branches.

Most spectacular of all is *W.f.* 'Multijuga' AGM (syn. *W.f.* 'Macrobotrys') which has the longest racemes of pale lilac-blue flowers shaded purple from 0.3–0.8m long. There are white forms of both species and quite a number of named cultivars such as *W.f.* 'Rosea' AGM (syn. *W.* 'Pink Ice') with pale rose flowers; *W.f.* 'Purple Patches' (syn. *W.f.* 'Murasaki-naga') with long racemes of violet-purple flowers; and *W.f.* 'Kuchi-beni' (syn. *W.f.* 'Peaches and Cream'), rose-pink buds opening virtually white.

Wisteria sinensis

YUCCA

The sharp sword-shaped leaves of *Yucca* provide a complete contrast in form to most other shrubs. The 75cm high leaves of *Yucca filamentosa* AGM grow from soil level and, as the name suggest, white threads form on their edges. *Yucca gloriosa* AGM produces a short trunk with a rosette of leaves to 2m. There are good variegated leaf forms of both and all produce large flower spikes up to 1m tall.

Y. filamentosa flowers in 2–3 years in July/August while *Y. gloriosa* takes five years or so to flower in September or October. The stories that these plants grow, flower and die are a fallacy, as is the suggestion that they only flower once every seven years.

Yucca filamentosa

Cultivation

Wisteria do not take kindly to root disturbance and for speedy establishment container-grown plants are a must.

If newly-transplanted specimens are slow to break into growth, spray the stems with water and be patient.

All soils, from heavy clay to quite light and sandy, are acceptable, the strongest growth coming in moist, fertile conditions. A sheltered site and the protection of a south or west-facing wall prevents wind and late frosts damaging the flowers. It is possible to train single stems up to form a trunk and with regular pinching a free-standing tree with pendant flowers.

Propagation is by seed of the species although seedlings can be very slow to flower, and by grafting. Grafted named varieties will cost more but are well worth the extra for their earlier flowering alone.

Pruning can be done twice a year – in early summer all side growths can be regularly pinched back to six leaves and then in winter these shortened laterals are cut back to 2–4cm to form flowering spurs.

Cultivation

These specimens are hardy in Britain and the most free-flowering will occur in well-drained sunny positions.

Propagate *Yucca* from suckers dug off in March/April and re-planted immediately.

Index of Common Names

Alexandrian Laurel, see *Danae*, 66
Barberry, see *Berberis*, 39
Bay, see *Laurus*, 86
Beauty Bush, see *Kolkwitzia*, 85
Blue Spiraea, see *Caryopteris*, 48
Blueberry, see *Vaccinium*, 123
Boston Ivy, see *Parthenocissus*, 96
Bottle Brush, see *Callistemon*, 45
Box Elder, see *Acer*, 32
Box, see *Buxus*, 44
Boxwood, see *Buxus*, 44
Bramble, see *Rubus*, 111
Broom, see *Genista*, 75
Buffalo Currant, see *Ribes*, 109
Butcher's Broom, see *Ruscus*, 112
Butterfly Bush, see *Buddleia*, 42
Calico Bush, see *Kalmia*, 84
Californian Lilac, see *Ceanothus*, 49
Californian Poppy, see *Romneya*, 109
Cedar Gum, see *Eucalyptus*, 70
Cherry Laurel, see *Prunus*, 102
Chinese Gooseberry, see *Actinidia*, 34
Christmas Box, see *Sarcococca*, 115
Cotton Lavender, see *Santolina*, 115
Cranberry, see *Vaccinium*, 123
Currant Tree, see *Amelanchier*, 34
Dogwood, see *Cornus*, 56
Elderberry, see *Sambucus*, 114
False-Caster-Oil-Plant, see *Fatsia*, 72
Firethorn, see *Pyracantha*, 104
Flowering Currant, see *Ribes*, 109
Golden Nut, see *Corylus*, 58
Granny's Curls, see *Leycesteria*, 87
Guelder Rose, see *Viburnum*, 124
Gum, see *Eucalyptus*, 70
Harry Lauder's Walking Stick,
  see *Corylus*, 58
Hazel, see *Corylus*, 58
Holly, see *Ilex*, 82

Honeysuckle, see *Lonicera*, 90
Ivy, see *Hedera*, 78
Japanese Lantern, see *Leycesteria*, 87
Japanese Quince, see *Chaenomeles*, 50
Japonica, see *Chaenomeles*, 50
Jew's Mallow, see *Kerria*, 84
Judas Tree, see *Cercis*, 50
Kiwi Fruit, see *Actinidia*, 34
Lace Cap, see *Hydrangea*, 80
Larustinus, see *Viburnum*, 124
Laurel, see *Laurus*, 86
Lavender, see *Lavandula*, 86
Ling, see *Heather*, 76
Maple, see *Acer*, 32
May, see *Crataegus*, 63
Mexican Orange Blossom, see *Choisya*, 52
Mile-a-Minute, see *Fallopia*, 72
Mock Orange, see *Philadelphus*, 98
Mop Head, see *Hydrangea*, 80
Myrtle, see *Myrtus*, 95
New Zealand Holly, see *Olearia*, 95
Oregon Grape, see *Mahonia*, 94
Privet, see *Ligustrum*, 88
Quickthorn, see *Crataegus*, 63
Rock Rose, see *Cistus*, page 53
Rose of Sharon, see *Hypericum*, 81
Rosemary, see *Rosmarinus*, 111
Rue, see *Ruta*, 111
Russian Vine, see *Fallopia*, 72
Russian Sage, see *Perovskia*, 97
Sage, see *Salvia*, 113
Scarlet Haw, see *Crataegus*, 63
Sea Buckthorn, see *Hippophae*, 79
Sheep Laurel, see *Kalmia*, 84
Shrubby Germander, see *Teucrium*, 122
Smoke Tree/Bush, see *Cotinus*, 59
Smooth Sumach, see *Rhus*, 108
Snowberry, see *Symphoricarpos*, 120
Snowy Mespilus, see *Amelanchier*, 34

Spanish Broom, see *Spartium*, 117
Spanish Gorse, see *Cytisus*, 75
Spindle Tree, see *Euonymus*, 70
Spotted Laurel, see *Aucuba*, 35
St. John's Wort, see *Hypericum*, 81
Stag's Horn Sumach, See *Rhus*, 108
Strawberry Tree, see *Arbutus*, 35
Sumach, see *Rhus*, 108
Sun Rose, see *Cistus*, 53
Sycamore, see *Acer*, 32
Thornless Silver Berry, see *Elaeagnus*, 68
Tree Poppy, see *Romneya*, 109
Tree Hollyhock, see *Hibiscus*, 79
Venetian Sumach, see *Cotinus*, 59
Veronica, see *Hebe*, 78
Virginia Creeper, see *Parthenocissus*, 96
Willow, see *Salix*, 112
Winter Sweet, see *Chimonanthus*, 52
Wire-netting Bush, see *Corokia*, 58
Witch Hazel, see *Hamamelis*, 76
Woodbine, see *Lonicera*, 90

**See Contents, page 5, for page
references to cultivation, usage etc.**